Ordnance Survey

Perthshire
Walks

Pathfinder Guide

Compiled by John Watney   Series editor: Brian Conduit

Key to colour coding

The walks are divided into three broad categories, indicated by the following colours:

Short, easy walks

Walks of moderate length, likely to involve some uphill walking

More challenging walks, which may be longer and/or over more rugged terrain, of ten with some stiff climbs

Acknowledgements

I should like to thank the following people for their help in the production of this guide: Brian Brookes, Highland Field Studies, Dunkeld; the Factor's Office of the Atholl Estate; the Forestry Commission Office in Dunkeld; Clive Kent, Director of Planning of Perth and Kinross District Council; John McKenna of Auchterarder; Martin Robinson, RSPB Warden at Balrobbie Farm; Lou Skinner of Pitlochry; the staff of the tourist information offices in Aberfeldy, Auchterarder, Blairgowrie, Crieff, Dunkeld and Pitlochry; Peter Littwin of Crieff for valuable research on the ground and the many local people and walkers met on the way.

While every care has been taken to ensure the accuracy of the route directions, the publishers cannot accept responsibility for errors or omissions, or for changes in details given. It has to be emphasised that the countryside is not static: hedges and fences can be removed, field boundaries can alter, footpaths can be rerouted and changes of ownership can result in the closure or diversion of some concessionary paths. Also paths that are easy and pleasant for walking in fine conditions may become slippery, muddy and difficult in wet weather and stepping stones over rivers and streams may become impassable. If readers know of any changes which have taken place, or have noticed any inaccuracies, Jarrold Publishing would be grateful to hear from them.

Ordnance Survey   ISBN 0-319-00371-X
Jarrold Publishing ISBN 0-7117-0673-5

First published 1994 by Ordnance Survey and Jarrold Publishing

Ordnance Survey   Jarrold Publishing
Romsey Road   Whitefriars
Maybush   Norwich NR3 1TR
Southampton SO9 4DH

Printed in Great Britain by Jarrold Printing, Norwich, 1/94

Previous page: *White Church, Comrie, seen across the River Earn*

Contents

Introduction to Perthshire

When seen from the A9 north of Stirling, the Grampian Mountains fill the horizon in a great arc from the Trossachs in the west to beyond Glenshee and Ballater in the north-east. Perthshire, it would seem, is all mountain country, and that is certainly true of its northern half. But much of the area is low-lying, with flat woodland and agricultural land bordered by the gentle, rounded downs of the Ochil Hills.

Hillwalking country

Walkers need go no further north than Perthshire for landscapes as varied and inspiring as can be found anywhere else in Scotland. Within a compact 2,000 square miles (5,180 sq km), laced with good roads, they have a choice of mountains, moorlands and gentle hills, forests and wooded glens, great lakes and little lochans, Roman roads and country lanes, castles, and neolithic and Celtic sites.

The Highland Fault, which lies diagonally across the country, divides the lowlands from the southern Highlands, which have formed a geographical barrier that has influenced the course of Scottish history since the time of Agricola. While the southern Highlands have their share of Munros – mountains over 3,000 feet

(915 m) – and innumerable ranges just below that mark, they are of gentler shape than most of those found north of the Great Glen with their steep corries, scree slopes, rock buttresses, sharp, bare peaks and greater heights. Almost every Perthshire mountain is grass-clad to its summit, which is likely to be flat and may even be grazed by sheep. It is hillwalking rather than climbing country – and one of its most pleasant characteristics is its overall greenness from the tips of its summits to its valley floors with, come late summer, great blankets of purple heather on hillside and moor. But the weather can be fickle.

If there is the slightest chance of cloud or mist coming down, no attempt should be made on summits or high ridges without a map and compass and the ability to use them. It is always colder and the wind blows harder on the tops than in the valleys. The experienced hillwalker will carry a day sack with extra warm and waterproof clothes and quick-energy food.

Historic landscape

Four thousand years ago Perthshire, like most of Scotland, was covered by dense forest. Then man began to clear the land for tilling and grazing. Defensive sites, settlements and the roads between them meant the destruction of more trees, and then the axe climbed higher to fell trees for building and smelting. With the disappearance of the forests the high

Cloan House – a Scottish baronial seat – at the start of Walk 8 in Cloan Glen

ground was used for summer grazing. The cattle were accompanied by the women and children who lived in shielings, the ruins of which now dot the landscape; many of the paths now so useful to hillwalkers were drove roads and service roads to the shielings. They were abandoned after the clearances, when sheep replaced cattle on the hills.

Meanwhile, trees returned to the lower slopes. In the late eighteenth century Sir Duncan Campbell began planting the bare slopes of Drummond Hill above Kenmore. He started the fashion for tree-planting over the next century. The greatest planters were the Dukes of Atholl, who owned some 500 square miles (1,300 sq km) and who planted over 15,000 acres (6,070 ha) with 14 million larches, happily also together with oaks, Scots pines and other species. We have them to thank for the beautiful forested vales through which the A9 runs from Dunkeld to Blair Atholl with its network of woodland trails, most notably Hermitage Walk at Dunkeld and the riverside path through the Pass of Killiecrankie.

Great swathes of forest are now owned by the Forestry Commission, who are continually developing their parkland to enhance the landscape, encourage wild-life and provide recreational amenities in tandem with producing timber. With their open access policy, they provide hundreds of miles of walks. The National Trust for Scotland have also laid out trails through their forest properties, and there are in addition many thousands of acres of private forest and woodland with permissive paths for walkers.

Another attraction for the walker is the county's multitude of hidden hillside glens with their fast running streams and waterfalls. Many have well-maintained paths with strategically sited walkways against sheer, tree-hung rockfaces, with viewing platforms overlooking them. All paths are picturesque, with interesting plant and animal life, and some are accessible to the disabled. A few have demanding gradients, but these lead onto high walks or to mountain passes into neighbouring valleys.

Perthshire has enough scenic lochs to vie with Cumbria's Lake District but does not seem to be so busy in the summer months. To the north and west lie the magnificent lochs Earn, Rannoch and Tay, long, deep stretches of water, cradled by steep mountain slopes. The western end of Loch Rannoch reaches almost to the edge of Rannoch Moor, one of Europe's last true wildernesses. Its north shore provides the finest views of the perfect

conical summit of Schiehallion, arguably Scotland's prettiest mountain. Along its south shore, remnants of the ancient Caledonian Forest are found in the Black Wood of Rannoch. Further west, Loch Tummel provides one of the most popular panoramic views in Scotland, the Queen's View, from a small pulpit of rock above the water, which is often packed with tourists. From there a number of walks head up into Tummel Forest where there are less crowded views down the loch.

Loch Tay is the largest of the lochs, 14 miles (22.5 km) long, with the highest mountain in Perthshire, Ben Lawers, towering 3,981 feet (1,213 m) over its northern shore. The southern shore is most picturesque, with a string of hamlets snuggling at the bottom of glens. Kenmore, at the foot of the loch, is a model village by the entrance to Taymouth Castle and park, where there is a beautifully landscaped golf-course, overlooked by Drummond Hill, which itself has the distinction of being Scotland's first managed forest. The River Tay leaves the loch to snake its way through the heart of the county, through Perth and Dundee, to make its escape into the North Sea 119 miles (191 km) later. Along the banks of the Tay ancient man has left his standing stones and circles. Later came landowners who built castles and mansions – monuments to their wealth. Here too is Scotland's ancient religious centre, Dunkeld. A good road runs along most of the river's length, ensuring that today's tourists have the chance to enjoy its many moods. As a prime salmon river the Tay attracts anglers from all over the world, so contributing greatly to the local economy.

The Grampians tower over Loch Earn, in particular Ben Vorlich and Stùc a' Chroin, two Munros at 3,224 feet (982 m) and 3,189 feet (972 m). This is a popular boating and fishing centre. St Fillans at its eastern extremity is an old-established holiday village with some fine villas hiding on the hills above. Here it was that the first Irish missionaries came, and the village is named after the best known of them. It was also the furthest point of the Roman penetration into the Highlands and from where they were turned back.

Between Dunkeld and Blairgowrie lie some of the prettiest of small lochs surrounded by green fields and woodland. One is Loch Lowes, an important nature reserve, with hides for visitors. Another is Loch Leven by Kinross, which is a bird sanctuary with an island, Castle Island, where Mary Queen of Scots was held

Samson's Stone, left behind above Strathearn by the last Ice Age, is seen on Walk 20

prisoner. And there are countless lochans, tucked away like little jewels in the folds of the hills.

Strathearn, Breadalbane and Atholl

Perthshire can be divided into distinctive divisions, both geographical and historical. Strathearn takes in the wide valley of the Earn, from Lochearnhead to Bridge of Earn where it flows into the Tay, and includes the glens and their little rivers which feed it. Here, the largest town is the holiday resort of Crieff, although Auchterarder, with the world-famous Gleneagles Hotel beside it, is the official capital. From the Ochil Hills in the southwest or from the high ground above Crieff, some 200 square miles (520 sq km) of the strath's fertile land of pastures and old parkland can be seen spread out like a picnic blanket.

Wherever you walk there are reminders of the past. Almost every hill of any importance has at least the vestiges of some prehistoric defensive settlement or fort and, most prolific in Strathearn, are the sites of the early Irish Celtic Church and Pictish stones carved with both pre- and post-Christian symbols. The Romans also left behind traces of their forts and signal stations, and there are still a few lengths of straight Roman road which can be walked.

Around the small town of Braco, just off the A9 before Auchterarder, is an area which was for a while occupied by the Romans at the time of Agricola's most northerly advance. There are a number of

Roman sites, forts and camps now grassed over, but their outlines are discernible, and the most important one at Braco itself shows clearly defined ditches. Braco looks across Strathearn to the beginning of the Highlands, and one can imagine Agricola's frustration at this natural barrier to his ambitions. Crieff is an important holiday town – a good base for a number of walks along the River Earn and up into the hills to the summit of Ben Chonzie and over to Loch Tay.

In the north are the divisions of Breadalbane and Atholl, both relatively vast and mountainous.

Breadalbane stretches from the former Argyll eastwards to Glen Almond, Aberfeldy and Strath Tay. It is nearly 1,000 square miles (2,590 sq km) in extent and encompasses the whole basin of the upper Tay, including the great loch. Aberfeldy is its largest town, although Killin at the western end of Loch Tay was the ancient capital, where the Cambells ruled from Finlarig Castle. In 1681 a Campbell became the 1st Earl of Breadalbane, and his descendants became the biggest landowners in Scotland, from the east to the west coast and taking in most of the Central Highlands. They no longer own an acre of that land, and the empty Taymouth Castle at Kenmore is their sad memorial.

In the far north is Atholl where lie the tourist centres of Dunkeld, Pitlochry, Killiecrankie and Blair Atholl, which have some of the most scenic and pleasant walks in the county. Blair Castle, seat of the Dukes of Atholl, is possibly the greatest tourist attraction in Scotland. A white-washed, fairy-tale building, it has thirty-two rooms full of beautiful treasures to amaze and delight visitors. When it rains, as unfortunately it so often does in the Highlands, it is no punishment to spend the best part of a day among the pictures and furniture, arms, uniforms, trophies, tapestries, china and glassware in this great castle. The estate stretches north up into the Forest of Atholl, now an almost bare mountain country, dominated by 3,307-foot (1,008 m) Beinn Dearg.

Quality and tranquillity

Queen Victoria and Sir Walter Scott made the area fashionable, and it has been accustomed to receiving visitors for some 150 years, so wherever you choose to walk there is probably a small town or village nearby long devoted to looking after the creature comforts and entertainment of travellers.

This is very much a rural county, with lots of charming villages, but only one big town, the City of Perth. There is no great industry apart from whisky-distilling, and there is plenty of that. In fact at least a day or two could be spent doing nothing but visiting distilleries and sampling their products. There are, though, many small-scale craft industries catering mostly to visitors, particularly the several working water mills for meal-milling and wool-weaving, as well as potters, glass-blowers and bagpipe-makers demonstrating their skills. The towns, though small, all have a sprinkling of quality shops selling woollen goods, the ubiquitous tartans, malt whiskies and excellent local food and preserves. Perthshire also offers its visitors all types of accommodation –

The top of Black Spout falls on Edradour Burn

renowned hotels, bed-and-breakfast establishments, self-catering chalets, hostels, and camping and caravan sites.

Perthshire's scenery and the peace and tranquillity in the glens and on the hills are its most valuable assets, and this has not changed all that much since Sir Walter Scott wrote: 'If an intelligent stranger were asked to describe the most varied and most beautiful province in Scotland, it is probable that he would name the county of Perth.'

The law and tradition as they affect walking in Scotland

Walkers following the routes given in this book should not run into problems, but it is as well to know something about the law as it affects access, and also something of the traditions which can be quite different in Scotland from elsewhere in Britain. Most of it is common sense, observing the country code and having consideration for other people and their activities which, after all, may be their livelihood.

It is often said that there is no law of trespass in Scotland. In fact there is, but the trespass itself is not a criminal offence. You can be asked to leave any property, and technically 'reasonable force' may be used to obtain your compliance – though the term is not defined! You can be charged with causing damage due to the trespass, but this would be hard to establish if you were just walking on open, wild, hilly country where, whatever the law, in practice there has been a long tradition of free access for recreational walking – something both the Scottish Landowners' Federation and the Mountaineering Council of Scotland do not want to see changed.

There are certain restrictions. Walkers should obey the country code and seasonal restrictions arising from lambing or stalking priorities. Where there is any likelihood of such restrictions this is mentioned in the text, and visitors are asked to comply. When camping, use one of Lochaber's many campsites. Camp fires should not be lit; they are a danger to moorland and forest and really not necessary as lightweight and efficient stoves are now available.

In theory a persistent trespasser or someone proving a nuisance (camping or causing vandalism) can be restrained by interdict – the Scots term for the placing of a court order banning certain actions.

In reality there is no way any law can be enforced completely in the huge, empty landscape of the Highlands, and legal action is almost unheard of; the system of *de facto* tolerance and mutual respect seems to have worked well. But it does depend on the visitor knowing the rules, written and unwritten, observing restraint during the stalking season, and following the country code.

Many of the walks in this book are on rights of way. In Scotland rights of way are not marked on the Ordnance Survey maps as is the case south of the border. Local planning authorities however have a duty to protect and maintain them – no easy task with limited resources. In the Highlands nearly every major glen or lochside will be a right of way, and it was not felt necessary to show these as such on the maps – a further reflection of the greater freedom to roam that is enjoyed in Scotland. The only established rights of way are those where a court case has resulted in a legal judgment. No major attempt at closing claimed rights of way has ever been successful, though several cases have gone to the Court of Session and even the House of Lords.

So a path on a map is no indication of a right of way, and many paths and tracks of great use to walkers were built by estates as stalking-paths or for private access. While you may traverse such paths taking due care to avoid damage to property and the natural environment, you should obey restricted access notices and if asked to leave do so. In Scotland (on rights of way) a cycle is regarded as 'an aid to pedestrianism'. A dog on a lead or under control may also be taken on a right of way. There is little chance of meeting a free-range solitary bull on any of the walks. Any herds seen are not likely to be dairy cattle, but all cows can be inquisitive and approach walkers, especially if they have a dog. Dogs running among stock may be shot on the spot; this is not draconian legislation but a desperate attempt to stop sheep and lambs being harmed, driven to panic, or lost, sometimes with fatal results. Any practical points or restrictions applicable will be made in the text. If there is no comment it can be assumed that the route carries no real restrictions.

The watchdog on rights of way in Scotland is the Scottish Rights of Way Society (SRWS), who maintain details on all established cases and will, if need be, contest attempted closures. They produce a booklet on the Scottish legal position (*Rights of Way, A Guide to the Law in Scotland*, 1991), and their green signposts are a familiar sight by many a Highland road, indicating the lines of historic routes.

Scotland in fact likes to keep everything as natural as possible, so, for instance, waymarking is kept to a minimum (the

Taymouth Castle, below Drummond Hill, where Queen Victoria stayed on her honeymoon

Scottish Rights of Way Society signposts and Forest Walk markers are in unobtrusive colours). In Scotland people are asked to 'walk softly in the wilderness, to take nothing, except photographs, and leave nothing except footprints' – which is better than any law.

Glossary of Gaelic names

Most of the place-names in this region are Gaelic in origin, and this list gives some of the more common elements, which will allow readers to understand otherwise meaningless words and appreciate the relationship between place-names and landscape features. Place-names often have variant spellings, and the more common of these are given here.

For a more detailed list refer to Drummond, P., *Scottish Hill and Mountain Names* (Scottish Mountaineering Trust, 1991) and the Ordnance Survey's booklet *Place Names on Maps of Scotland and Wales* (1981).

A view between rowan-trees near Amulree

aber	mouth of loch, river
abhainn	river
allt	stream
auch, ach	field
bal, bail, baile	town, homestead
bàn	white, fair, pale
bealach	hill pass
beg, beag	small
ben, beinn	hill
bhuidhe	yellow
blar	plain
brae, braigh	upper slope, steepening
breac	speckled
cairn	pile of stones, often marking a summit
cam	crooked
càrn	cairn, cairn-shaped hill
caol, kyle	strait
ceann, ken, kin	head
cil, kil	church, cell
clach	stone
clachan	small village
cnoc	hill, knoll, knock
coille, killie	wood
corrie, coire, choire	mountain hollow
craig, creag	cliff, crag
crannog, crannag	man-made island
dàl, dail	field, flat
damh	stag
dearg	red
druim, drum	long ridge
dubh, dhu	black, dark
dùn	hill fort
eas	waterfall
eilean	island
eilidh	hind
eòin, eun	bird
fionn	white
fraoch	heather
gabhar, ghabhar, gobhar	goat
garbh	rough
geal	white
ghlas, glas	grey
gleann, glen	narrow, valley
gorm	blue, green
inbhir, inver	confluence
inch, inis, innis	island, meadow by river
lag, laggan	hollow
làrach	old site
làirig	pass
leac	slab
liath	grey
loch	lake
lochan	small loch
màm	pass, rise
maol	bald-shaped top
monadh	upland, moor
mór, mor(e)	big
odhar, odhair	dun-coloured
rhu, rubha	point
ruadh	red, brown
sgòr, sgòrr, sgùrr	pointed
sron	nose
stob	pointed
strath	valley (broader than glen)
tarsuinn	traverse, across
tom	hillock (rounded)
tòrr	hillock (more rugged)
tulloch, tulach	knoll
uisge	water, river

Key Map 1

SCALE 1: 250 000 or 4 MILES to 1 INCH

Key Map 2

SCALE 1: 250 000 or 4 MILES to 1 INCH

CONVENTIONAL SIGNS 1 : 25 000 or 2½ INCHES to 1 MILE

ROADS AND PATHS
Not necessarily rights of way

M1 or A6(M)	M1 or A6(M)	Motorway
A 31(T)	A 31(T)	Trunk or Main road
B 3074	B 3074	Secondary road
A 35	A 35	Dual carriageway
		Road generally more than 4m wide
		Road generally less than 4m wide
		Other road, drive or track

Unfenced roads and tracks are shown by pecked lines

.... Path

RAILWAYS

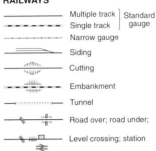

Multiple track	⎫ Standard
Single track	⎭ gauge
Narrow gauge	
Siding	
Cutting	
Embankment	
Tunnel	
Road over; road under;	
Level crossing; station	

PUBLIC RIGHTS OF WAY Public rights of way may not be evident on the ground

} Public paths { Footpath
Bridleway

+ + + + + Byway open to all traffic
▲ ▼ ▲ ▼ Road used as a public path

DANGER AREA
Firing and test ranges in the area
Danger!
Observe warning notices

The indication of a towpath in this book does not necessarily imply a public right of way
The representation of any other road, track or path is no evidence of the existence of a right of way
Public rights of way are not shown on Ordnance Survey maps of Scotland

BOUNDARIES

— · — · — · —	County (England and Wales)	Coincident boundaries are shown by the first appropriate symbol
— — — —	District	
—○—○—○—	London Borough	*For Ordnance Survey purposes CountyBoundary is deemed to be the limit of the parish structure whether or not a parish area adjoins
....	Civil Parish (England)* Community (Wales)	
— — — — —	Constituency (County, Borough, Burgh or European Assembly)	

SYMBOLS

⌘ ⌘ ⌘	Place of worship	with tower
		with spire, minaret or dome
		without such additions
☐ ☐	Building; important building	
▓ △	Glasshouse; youth hostel	
▦	Bus or coach station	
☒ ☒	Lighthouse; beacon	
△ ▲	Triangulation pillar	
. T; A; R	Telephone: public; AA; RAC	
▩▩▩▩	Sloping masonry	
---□----....	Electricity transmission line	
pylon pole		
○ W, Spr	Well, Spring	
⌖	Site of antiquity	
✕ 1066	Site of battle (with date)	

Gravel pit	
Other pit or quarry	
Sand pit	
Refuse or slag heap	
Loose rock	
Outcrop	
Cliff	
Boulders	
Scree	

☐ Water		☐ Mud
☐	Sand; sand & shingle	
▨	National Park or Forest Park Boundary	
NT	National Trust always open	
NT	National Trust limited access, observe local signs	
NTS NTS	National Trust for Scotland	
FC	Forestry Commission	

VEGETATION Limits of vegetation are defined by positioning of the symbols but may be delineated also by pecks or dots

♣ ♣	Coniferous trees	○ ○ ○ Orchard
○ ○ ○	Non-coniferous trees	Scrub
⬡ ⬡	Coppice	Marsh, reeds, saltings.

Bracken, rough grassland ⎫
In some areas bracken (⊓) and rough grassland (......) are shown separately ⎬ Shown collectively as rough grassland on some sheets
Heath ⎭

In some areas reeds (∾) and saltings (∿) are shown separately

HEIGHTS AND ROCK FEATURES

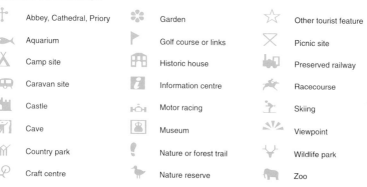

50
285
} Determined by { ground survey
air survey

Surface heights are to the nearest metre above mean sea level. Heights shown close to a triangulation pillar refer to the ground level height at the pillar and not necessarily at the summit

Vertical face

Loose rock   Boulders   Outcrop   Scree

Contours are at 5 metres vertical interval

TOURIST INFORMATION

✝	Abbey, Cathedral, Priory	✽	Garden	☆	Other tourist feature
🐟	Aquarium	⚑	Golf course or links	✕	Picnic site
⚊	Camp site	🏛	Historic house	🚂	Preserved railway
🚐	Caravan site	𝒊	Information centre	🏇	Racecourse
🏰	Castle	⊙	Motor racing	⛷	Skiing
🏚	Cave	🖼	Museum	☀	Viewpoint
🏛	Country park	❗	Nature or forest trail	🦌	Wildlife park
⚘	Craft centre	🦆	Nature reserve	🐂	Zoo
🅿	Parking				
PC	Public Convenience (in rural areas)				

𝔐 Ancient Monuments and Historic Buildings in the care of the Secretary of State for the Environment which are open to the public

◆ ◆ National trail or Recreational Path Long Distance Route (Scotland only)

Pennine Way Named path

Cross SAILING Selected places of interest

 T Public Telephone

⊕ Mountain rescue post

NATIONAL PARK ACCESS LAND Boundary of National Park access land Private land for which the National Park Planning Board have negotiated public access

◄ Access Point

WALKS

🖉 1 Start point of walk   Featured walk   ➤ Route of walk   ▪▪▶▪ Alternative route

ABBREVIATIONS

1 : 25 000 or 2½ INCHES to 1 MILE also 1 : 10 000/1 : 10 560 or 6 INCHES to 1 MILE

BP,BS	Boundary Post or Stone	Mon	Monument	Spr	Spring
CH	Club House	P	Post Office	T	Telephone, public
FV	Ferry Foot or Vehicle	Pol Sta	Police station	A,R	Telephone, AA or RAC
FB	Foot Bridge	PC	Public Convenience	TH	Town Hall
HO	House	PH	Public House	Twr	Tower
MP,MS	Mile Post or stone	Sch	School	W	Well
				Wd Pp	Wind Pump

Abbreviations applicable only to 1 : 10 000/1 : 10 560 or 6 INCHES to 1 MILE

Ch	Church	P	Pole or Post	TCB	Telephone Call Box
F Sta	Fire Station	PW	Place of Worship	TCP	Telephone Call Post
Fn	Fountain	S	Stone	Y	Youth Hostel
GP	Guide Post				

FOLLOW THE COUNTRY CODE

Enjoy the countryside and respect its life and work

Guard against all risk of fire

Fasten all gates

Keep your dogs under close control

Keep to public paths across farmland

Leave livestock, crops and machinery alone

Use gates and stiles to cross fences, hedges and walls

Take your litter home

Help to keep all water clean

Protect wildlife, plants and trees

Take special care on country roads

Make no unnecessary noise

Reproduced by permission of the Countryside Commission for Scotland

1 Black Spout Wood

Start:	Signpost on Perth Road, Pitlochry
Distance:	1½ miles (3 km)
Approximate time:	1¾ hours
Parking:	Car park by railway bridge off the Perth Road
Refreshments:	Hotels, restaurants, pubs and cafés in Pitlochry
Ordnance Survey maps:	Landranger 52 (Pitlochry & Aberfeldy), Pathfinder 309 NN 85/95 (Pitlochry)

General description *This is a pleasant stroll through a mainly oak-wood to an unexpected ancient Pictish site, an impressive waterfall and the offer of a free drink at a distillery. There are lots of wild flowers on the way, and just sufficient gradients to provide a little exercise. It may be a bit muddy in parts after rain, but no special footwear is required. It is perfect as a first-day warm-up walk before making longer sorties into the nearby glens and hills or, being only minutes from the town centre, a post-prandial walk for those who have enjoyed a good meal at one of Pitlochry's Victorian hotels.*

Pitlochry is one of the most popular touring centres in Scotland, set as it is near the valleys of the Tay, Tummel and Garry. Despite the A9 bypass, there is still plenty of traffic along the main street, and mornings and evenings see coaches picking up and setting down their groups

```
0      200    400    600    800m    1 kilometre
0      200    400    600yds    ½ mile
SCALE 1:25 000 or 2½ INCHES to 1 MILE
```

of holidaymakers. The salmon ladder at the hydroelectric power station is a popular attraction, and this little town can be proud of the high standard of drama, ballet and concerts maintained by its Festival Theatre.

Follow Pitlochry's main street south into Perth Road, past the Royal Atholl Hotel drive and the sewage works to the Black Spout Wood signpost on the left. Pass under the railway bridge with the car park on the right. The walk starts up a soft-going grass path beside a rough road which once took lorries to the town rubbish dump, now filled in. This path goes alongside one corner of the Royal Atholl Hotel's golf-course to a T-junction with a sign pointing left to Pitlochry. Turn right here **(A)** and walk up as far as a wooden bench. The direct route to Black Spout waterfall is straight ahead, but bear right instead along an overgrown and extremely narrow path, distinguished by the half-buried stone drainage gutters crossing it at intervals.

You will soon come to a low stone circle covered with earth and ferns, shown as Homestead on the map **(B)**. This is the site of a Pictish fort, little known even to locals, which was named Black Castle of Edradour by Thomas Pennant (1726–98). The path cuts through its north-west side, and to the south-west much of the stonework has fallen down a gorge into the Edradour Burn below, but the circle is quite discernible if one stops to look. In places trees have grown through it, their roots dislodging the stones. It is one of many Fingalian castles in this area, their name deriving from a mythical hero, Fionn of Fianna. In Gaelic these castles are known as *caistealan na féinne*, and their remains may often be found where a place-name includes the word 'castle', as in nearby Glen Fincastle. The path continues upstream near the edge of the gorge for a while and then rises steeply to a wooden viewing platform, opposite Black Spout. This waterfall drops down a cleft in the rockface of the gorge for about 150 feet (46 m) in three stages. Its white water shines brightly against the lush foliage hiding the rock and, when the sun is in the right position, rainbows dance in the spray. Further up the path above the falls it is possible to clamber down a trodden track through the trees to the flat rocks over which the Edradour falls. With some battling through the undergrowth, one can walk along an old path beside the burn to another set of small falls 100 yards (91 m) upstream, but a return the same way has to be made back to the path proper.

A path through Black Spot Wood, outside Pitlochry, which passes by the site of a Pictish fort

Climb on through the woods to a junction with a signpost, left to Moulin, right to Edradour **(C)**. Take the latter route and walk between the gorge deep below on the right and an arable field on the left, across which the south face of Ben Vrackie, 2,758 feet (841 m), is visible, with the much-worn path to its summit. Also visible across the top of the golf-course is the bald summit of Craigower at 1,335 feet (407 m). This footpath ends beside the car park of the Edradour Distillery, the smallest in Scotland, which takes its water from the Edradour Burn. The low white-painted stone buildings with their bright-red doors are typical of rural Highland architecture. Visitors are welcome, and are rewarded with a hospitable dram. The mashing, fermenting and distilling are done in a building of little more than 2,000 square feet (186 sq m), producing a mere 19,800 gallons (90,000 litres) a year, equivalent to the weekly output of a big distillery. They make two blended whiskies for export only, and a malt which sells in a few outlets in this country. Their claim to fame is their House of Lords Whisky which can

be found only in the visitors' shop and the Palace of Westminster.

On leaving the distillery take the road to the left of the car park and turn right down Colivoulin Farm Road to the edge of Black Spout Wood. Passing into the wood through a small gate, one is reassured by a finger-post with a yellow arrow pointing the way, because the path this side of the burn is not much used, so none too obvious. It keeps along the very top edge of the wood beside a field where the air is scented with wild garlic, and in season one can feast on wild raspberries. The path meets an old cart-road, grassed over and lined with gorse, which plunges down to the right into the woods, but a short distance along branch to the left through a mixture of conifers and birch, and then make a right-hand bend straight downhill to the railway embankment. A track beside the embankment is covered with many wild flowers, among them forget-me-nots. The track meets Edradour Burn, and together they turn under a railway bridge and take you back onto the Perth Road about 60 yards (55 m) south of where you started **(D)**. □

17

2 Kinnoull Hill, Perth

Start:	Quarry car park by Corsiehill
Distance:	2³/₄ miles (3.75 km)
Approximate time:	1¹/₄ hours
Parking:	Quarry car park by Corsiehill
Refreshments:	Hotels, restaurants, pubs and cafés in Perth
Ordnance Survey maps:	Landranger L53 (Blairgowrie), Pathfinder 350 NO 02/12 (Perth & Area)

General description *This is a pleasant and not too strenuous walk to panoramic views overlooking the River Tay as it leaves Perth for Dundee and the sea. The route is selected as the most interesting of several waymarked through the woodlands of Kinnoull Hill, owned by Perth & Kinross District Council and the Forestry Commission. There is a gentle climb up about 700 feet (213 m) through birch and oak to a precipitous cliff top with views over the river towards the Ochil and*

Lomond hills. The summit is an area of Special Scientific Interest for its unusual plant life. The descent is made through heathland, being colonised by naturally regenerating woodland. There can be a few muddy places on the way after rain, but on the whole the walking is easy and does not require heavy footwear.

The start is reached by leaving the city over the Perth Bridge, the A85, and keeping straight ahead up Lochie Brae to the Royal Murray Hospital gates where you turn right up Muirhall Road, then after ³/₄ mile (1.25 km) take the right-hand turn signposted to Corsiehill and Kinnoull Hill Woodland Walk. Turn right into Corsiehill Road and park either by the viewpoint indicator (**A**) or go into the disused quarry car park.

From the indicator there is a fine view over the northern half of Perth with the River Tay winding away north towards the Grampian massif. Walk back to the road junction (**B**) and turn right and right again up a lane, and at a post marked '3' (**C**) take the left-hand fork past the gable end of a barn and follow a wall to a gate marked 'Private'. Make a dog-leg past the gate and keep going along a narrow woodland track to meet a broad forest

The summit indicator on Kinnoull Hill above Perth identifies hills, peaks and glens over 360°

road which was the original carriage-drive to the summit of Kinnoull Hill. Follow an arrow to the left on a waymarked post along the forest road as it curves round through tall conifers to Forest Lodge (D) and the Jubilee car park.

Turn right along the metalled road which runs downhill to Kinfauns and almost immediately, following a yellow marker, enter the woods on the right through a gap by a gate and start the climb up through magnificent beech-trees to Kinnoull Tower. The broad path keeps near the edge of the woodland with sweeping views over bright-green fields sloping down to the River Tay. In the autumn the walker can enjoy fat blackberries on the first part of the leg. Approaching the summit, where the path divides take the left fork, signposted 'Tower'. Soon you come upon a bench seat on the eastern end of the escarpment above the Tay, and it is worth taking time to absorb the view of the river meandering towards Dundee through one of Scotland's richest agricultural vales. Fruit-growing was once the major industry, and the local apples were famous even in London. Now the area is mostly given over to grain crops.

From here the path runs so close to the near-vertical southern escarpment of Kinnoull Hill that signs warn of 'Dangerous cliffs'. Almost unexpectedly one comes upon Kinnoull Tower (E), a folly standing on the very edge of the cliff. It is indeed a folly, having been built by an earl of Kinnoull to simulate one of the romantic German castles perched above the Rhine, which he had much admired on his grand tour. From its windows the panorama downriver does have a passing likeness to a Rhine view. It is when looking the other way down a great gully that one gets the bigger surprise – a superb aerial perspective of the elegant geometry of the Kinfauns interchange and the slender Friarton Bridge.

From the tower the path dips down into the trees to turn up round the edge of Windy Ghoull (F), a great gully in the escarpment which produces multiple echoes, from the far side of which the tower can be seen in its true setting at the edge of a crag which hangs high above the roaring traffic of the busy A85. Beyond the gully one emerges onto a small plateau. On it is set a stone table at which the earl was wont to picnic with his friends. The site was well chosen for there is nothing to interrupt the views either straight down the vertiginous cliff face or to the distant countryside beyond the river.

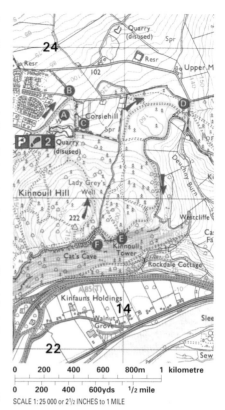

0   200   400   600   800m   1 kilometre

0   200   400   600yds   ¹/₂ mile

SCALE 1:25 000 or 2¹/₂ INCHES to 1 MILE

With binoculars on a clear day a great swathe of Perthshire from the Ochils to the Grampians can be studied in great detail. From the table, walk a few yards north to the summit triangulation pillar at 728 feet (222 m) and an orientation table identifying hills, peaks and glens over 360°. The hill, now a Site of Special Scientific Interest, was formed some 380 million years ago from volcanic lava and ash, and its dry surface provides favourable conditions for some unusual plants, chickweed wintergreen being an example.

From here the path winds downhill through a mixture of Scots pine, larch, Sitka spruce, Norway spruce, beech and rowan and some old oaks. The freshness of the air is indicated by the amount of grey 'beards' of lichen, much favoured by deer, which hang from the branches of the trees. Yellow posts keep you on the right track until the path reaches the disused quarry, just visible through the trees, and then the road.

Whether driving or walking, one can return to the city either back down the road to Perth Bridge or by turning left down Corsiehill Road to arrive down beside the river just south of the bridge. □

3 Glen Acharn, Loch Tay

Start:	Acharn
Distance:	3¼ miles (5 km)
Approximate time:	1½ hours
Parking:	Acharn
Refreshments:	None
Ordnance Survey maps:	Landranger 51 Loch Tay), Pathfinder 322 NN 64/74 (Ben Lawers & Lower Loch Tay)

General description *This is a short and easy uphill walk along the top of a glen to a strange cave, waterfalls, a tumulus and standing stones, then downhill back through woods above a noisy burn. The village of Acharn has a post office-cum-cottage shop and nothing else by way of facilities, but it is prettily placed on Loch Tay, 2 miles (3.25 km) from Kenmore.*

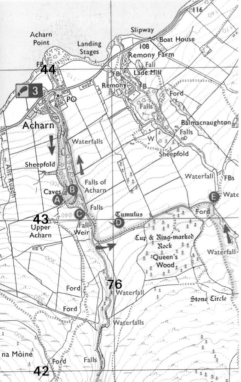

SCALE 1:25 000 or 2½ INCHES to 1 MILE

Acharn was one of six villages built by the 4th Earl of Breadalbane in the early 1800s to provide his estate workers with better housing.

Coming from the direction of Kenmore, cross the old stone bridge over the Acharn Burn and turn up a path on the left, signposted to the Falls of Acharn. This is a farm track with the burn hidden in a deep, tree-filled ravine on one side and rough fields sloping away uphill on the other. There are views back over Loch Tay to the eastern summits of the Ben Lawers massif. After passing a track to a sheepfold on the right, look out for the entrance on the left to a cave known as The Hermitage (**A**). You will need to bend low to crawl inside along a winding passage to come out on a rock ledge overlooking the Falls of Acharn in a steep-cut gorge at your feet. Walkers who do not wish to enter the cave can continue on up the track. The water falls over stepped ledges and at the bottom is split by a massive boulder, causing twin falls into a dark, peaty pool. Find your way back again in the dark through the Y-shaped cave to the open air a little further up the track. After no more than 200 yards (183 m), a sign points the way down a footpath to a viewpoint (**B**). This is actually a recently built complex of wooden walkways and a bridge (not shown on the map) over the burn, just below a point where it comes down a curved leat in the rock, like a spout into a water butt. Below the walkway the rock sides have been worn concave by the water, giving the sense of a cavern roofed over by hanging beeches. Many varieties of fern, moss and lichen thickly cover the rockfaces.

Rather than returning the same way, cross the bridge and continue up a short footpath to the right on the opposite bank. This leads past the head of the spout and up to a gate onto a stone bridge (**C**), where the original track comes across the burn. Go through a large farm gate and walk to the right, keeping close to the side of the glen, round a grassy knoll to the left and on towards Queen's Wood plantation. Beside the path is a grass mound, which is a tumulus or burial site (**D**).

Keep going along the edge of the plantation towards Remony Burn but, just before reaching it, turn right up a track across grassland (**E**). After climbing about 240 feet (73 m), go through a gate in a drystone wall to view the remains of a stone circle on a hillock. Some stones are still standing but most are lying down, and a stone dyke has been built across the site. It commands a view across Loch Tay to the southern flank of Schiehallion. From the stones, retrace your steps to the stone bridge over Acharn Burn and back through the small gate beside it which is signposted for Acharn. From here the path runs down the east side of the glen through the trees instead of above them and most of the time within sight of the burn below, passing through widely spaced beeches with their soft, crunchy floor, then through birches and finally some venerable oaks. At one point, look across the glen straight at the mouth of The Hermitage cave on its ledge above the waterfalls. The path emerges in the village beside the Old Meal Mill. It was here that a fugitive named Mackintosh sought refuge way back in history. The miller scattered flour over him and put a sieve in his hand, so when his pursuers arrived they found only the miller and his 'assistant' at work. The Crerar family in the village today are descendants of that fugitive. □

The pathside entrance to Hermitage Cave which leads to a view overlooking the Falls of Acharn

4 Killiecrankie Nature Reserve

Start: Balrobbie Farm, Killiecrankie

Distance: 3½ miles (5.5 km)

Approximate time: 2 hours

Parking: RSPB car park, Balrobbie Farm

Refreshments: Killiecrankie Hotel and Little Chef on old A9

Ordnance Survey maps: Landranger 43 (Braemar), Pathfinder 294 NN 86/96 (Blair Atholl & Killiecrankie)

General description *Killiecrankie Nature Reserve of 1,320 acres (534 ha) contains some of the best woodland in the area, including impressive crags, heather-covered moorland, birch- and larch-woods as well as farmland, providing habitats for a rich variety of flora and fauna. The RSPB manage the reserve, and they have unobtrusively marked out a circular trail which gives the walker access to all the most interesting parts. This unspoilt and largely wild country offers moderately strenuous exercise for the serious walker, with an ascent of about 1,000 feet (304 m) to superb summit views. The path is quite steep in places and will be muddy in wet weather so suitable footwear is essential, and because the natural balance of life is still so delicate on this reserve the RSPB do not allow dogs. Open every day from dawn to dusk, admission to the reserve is free, but there is a box for donations.*

The reserve is reached by leaving the A9 north of Pitlochry to continue on the B8079 to Killiecrankie and then taking the minor road on the left in the village over the River Garry and following the RSPB signs to Balrobbie Farm, where there is a car park and information board. Before leaving the farm, a moment should be taken to look at the landscape to the east. The highest peak on the right is Ben Vrackie, 2,758 feet (841 m), with a view-point indicator on its summit. It is a favourite hill walk of visitors to Pitlochry, and the way, which sadly is now worn almost 160 feet (50 m) wide in parts, goes up the south face which presents a much gentler slope than the steep and more dramatic face seen from the farm. In the valley immediately below Balrobbie Farm is the cluster of white houses of Killiecrankie at the head of the pass. It was on the hillslope above the village that the Battle of Killiecrankie was fought in 1689, a rare victory for the Jacobites over William III's troops. The battle started half an hour before sunset, and before dark 2,500 Highlanders on the high ground, led by the Earl of Dundee, had routed 4,000 troops below. Anyone who has read an account of the battle, or paid a visit to the Killiecrankie Visitor Centre, will be able to see it all happening again in their mind's eye as they look at the field of battle across the valley from Balrobbie Farm.

The walk starts by going back along the road from the farm and up the right fork **(A)**, instead of back to the village. This road runs parallel to 600-foot (183 m) crags whose faces are well covered with mixed broadleaf trees and crowned with larches. Jackdaws and a few stock doves nest in the rock crevices, where many rare plants grow in safety. Looking back along this way one sees the dome shape of Càrn Liath, 3,199 feet (975 m), to the north and behind it two of the pointed summits of Beinn a' Ghlo at 3,480 feet (1,061 m) and 3,703 feet (1,129 m). Leave the road through a gate marked with a yellow peg **(B)**, opposite Fonvuick Farm, and follow the path uphill. Just inside the gate there is a little waterlogged patch with a few examples of bogland plants. Crags stretch ahead for another ½ mile (0.75 km), and the walk climbs up alongside them and round the far end, reaching almost to the top. The way is easy to follow through the birch-woods, getting ever steeper as it nears the rockface. Beech fern, scaly male fern and lemon-scented fern are thick on the ground, and there is the chance of seeing woodpeckers, redstarts, tree-pipits and wood-warblers on the crags. Buzzards, kestrels and ravens occasionally nest in this woodland.

Breaks in the trees allow views over the new A9 as it runs on stilts along the lower slope of Meall Uaine with the more distant Ben Vrackie peering over its shoulder. At one point it is possible to count five peaks and at the same time look straight down onto the top of the little kirk at Tenandry nestling in the woods far below. Eventually the path winds round the end of the crags, after which the gradient flattens out into a sheltered basin planted with larches related to those on the Atholl estate. Here, if you go quietly, you may see roe-deer. The ground is now covered with heather and some swampy patches, and in season there will be wood crane's-bill, water

avens, marsh orchids and wintergreens. Above the basin, the ruins of a farmstead, Corhulichan **(C)** – marked but not named on the map – cling to the hillside. Only the walls remain, about 4 feet (1.2 m) high, with slightly higher gable ends. The main building, now a garden of ferns, is backed by a drystone-walled enclosure with old trees growing through its crumbled walls.

From the ruins the path climbs the last gradient through thick heather until the 1,312-foot (400 m) summit contour below Craig Fonvuick **(D)** is reached, marked by a solitary wind-burnt larch. The way to near Ardtulichan Farm is easy going, downhill along a wide path through the moorland heather. All the way down this hillside section there is a magnificent panoramic view of the River Garry wending its way down the Vale of Atholl with its fairy-tale white castle standing a little aloof from the village of Blair Atholl. The great hills of the Forest of Atholl, dominated by Beinn Dearg, a Munro of

Gateway to Killiecrankie Nature Reserve

3,307 feet (1,008 m), form a dramatic backdrop. Halfway down by a belt of birches a yellow marker indicates a steep path **(E)** down to the right. It is a rather fragile path and the going is difficult, so walkers are asked not to use it as a short-cut but to continue on towards the farm along a route now marked with green pegs. The path goes round the back of the farm and over a stile to meet the farm road. Follow it down beside Shelloch Den, a densely wooded ravine from which comes the faint sound of a hidden mountain burn. After a while the road emerges into open fields, where a green marker points to a footpath to the right, which leads to a stile **(F)** and thence to another ravine cut in the hillside. There is a small stream to jump over where a flat stone on the ground with a green arrow points the way up a narrow track through birch-woods. At this point there is a glimpse of Balrobbie Farm ahead.

The final leg is the prettiest part of the walk. Above the path, wet flushes – areas of earth enriched by chemicals that have leached out of rocks higher up and been washed down the hillside – support butterwort and yellow saxifrage. This an area of regeneration, and several plots are fenced off against the predations of livestock, deer, rabbits and hares. One such cage beside the path is dated 1986, so the rate of regeneration can be seen. The whole terrain over which one has walked is being carefully managed to support a natural plant population as well as bird life. Sheep have been taken off the high ground of the crags, while there is seasonal grazing on the lower slopes. □

5 Glen Lednock, Comrie

Start:	Comrie
Distance:	4 miles (6.5 km)
Approximate time:	3 hours
Parking:	Car park in Dundas Street, Comrie
Refreshments:	Hotel, restaurants and pubs in Comrie
Ordnance Survey maps:	Landranger 52 (Pitlochry & Aberfeldy), Pathfinder 348 NN 62/72 (Loch Earn & Comrie)

General description *This is a satisfying but gentle walk with just one short, steep and demanding climb. Starting from the eighteenth-century cottage weaving village of Comrie, which is in part an architectural conservation area, the first half of the walk is through a deep wooded glen to the sound of tumbling waters with small detours down to overviews of rapids and waterfalls. The way through the glen rises gently onto moorland before crossing over the river Lednock for the return journey through the pine-carpeted, dark and silent forest of Laggan Wood, hanging above the glen. For the less energetic, the moment for determination comes near the head of the glen where steps, and then a rocky zigzag path which might tax a mule, lead to Melville's Monument on the very edge of a crag at 859 feet (262 m). When the heart stops pounding, the magnificent views compensate for the effort made.*

Leaving the car park in Dundas Street, turn right and keep straight ahead past a telephone kiosk on the left and the traffic derestriction sign, just beyond which two stone pillars **(A)** mark the start of a woodland path signposted 'Glen Lednock Circular Walk and Deil's Caldron'. The path undulates through mixed woodland which clothes the near-vertical side of a ravine, from whence comes the sound of the rumbling water of the Lednock some 100 feet (30 m) below. Beech and Norway spruce compete with the remaining old coppiced oaks which 300 years ago filled the glen.

After a while the path descends nearer to the water until it passes a trodden way through the trees to the right down to a fenced-off viewpoint above the Little

Caldron **(B)**, a series of falls and rock pools; nothing dramatic but a pretty sight. Several other viewpoints in this area can be found along the rock ledges above the river. Regaining the original path, keep going as it rises up again to run alongside the minor road to Loch Lednock Reservoir. Do not exit onto the road but continue below the roadside wall to a wooden walkway recently built against a sheer rockface by 202 Field Squadron, Royal Engineers Volunteers. This walkway leads to a wooden staircase down to the Deil's Caldron (Devil's Kettle) **(C)** where the Lednock's waters are squeezed through a narrow-angled fissure in the rock and squirted out as a waterfall into a large kettle-shaped pothole, ground out by stones swirling round in the water. This spectacle is best seen when the sun is high so that the mouth of the dark fissure is illuminated.

From the Caldron, climb up the wooden staircase all the way to the road above, at which point one has to get one's breath

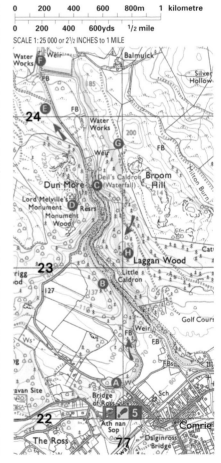

SCALE 1 : 25 000 or 2½ INCHES to 1 MILE

The River Lednock from Shaky Bridge on its way down to Comrie via the Deil's Caldron

before climbing some 400 feet (122 m) up to Dun More **(D)**, a crag on which stands a 75-foot- (23 m) high obelisk, a monument to Henry Dundas, 1st Viscount Melville, Lord Advocate for Scotland from 1775 to 1783 and a cabinet minister under William Pitt 'the Younger'. His friends erected it after his death in 1811. The steps are signposted to the monument, but they soon give way to a rocky track. Keeping a steady pace, the ascent can be made in about twenty minutes, but in wet weather the descent can be slippery and so may take almost as long. From the monument one gets an aerial view of Comrie huddled round its distinctive White Church, which could have been transported from an Alpine valley. Built in 1805, it is now a youth centre. To the west, a break in the range of hills gives a glimpse of Loch Earn, with the top of Ben Vorlich at 3,231 feet (985 m) in the distance, while nearby to the north is 3,048-foot- (929 m) high Ben Chonzie. In other directions half a dozen tops of well over 2,000 feet (610 m) can be identified on a clear day. Dun More stands on the edge of the Highlands, in fact on the side of the Highland Boundary Fault itself. In 1839 Comrie was shaken by a series of earth tremors which lasted for seven years, and the village became a tourist attraction as Scotland's 'earthquake capital'. In 1840 seismometers were set up there, the first in Europe.

Return to the road and keep going north. When the way bears left, go straight ahead on a farm track **(E)** slightly downhill to Shaky Bridge **(F)**, until recently a shaky wooden structure with one end lodged in the crook of a sycamore. Now, alas, those who know best have replaced it with a metal structure. Once over the bridge, turn right and walk downstream along the riverbank, which is lined with alders. In the eighteenth century these trees provided the wood for clog-making, and Comrie held an annual clog market in December. After a while the broad grass path narrows and climbs away from the river up towards a stile **(G)** over a stone wall into Laggan Wood. From here the woodland path is waymarked with little black men on wooden posts pointing the direction. After a short rise it is downhill all the way back to Comrie.

The wood is a mix of conifers, birch, larch and oak, so at times the path is dark and soft with a carpet of pine-needles, and in other parts it is sun-dappled, rough and bordered by moss-covered boulders. The path is all the time getting nearer the water, the sound of which gets louder, but before path and water meet there is a spur leading through a little oak-copse to a high point **(H)** with a seat overlooking Comrie. From that point, wooden steps take the path to a lower level, and eventually it arrives at the riverbank beside a weir. It is level-going from here on. The path ends beside a private garden, and a sign pointing to the village centre directs you down Nurse's Lane, actually past the district nurse's cottage, to a junction with Drummond Street, which is the A85, and the welcome sign 'Toilets 200 yards' (183 m), which is also the way back to the car park. Along Drummond Street there is the Scottish Tartans Museum to visit. Three rivers – the Lednock, the Water of Ruchill and the Earn – meet up in Comrie, hence its name which is derived from *conhruith*, meaning a 'confluence'. ☐

6 Braes of Fowlis, Strathearn

Start:	Fowlis Wester
Distance:	4½ miles (7.25 km)
Approximate time:	2½ hours
Parking:	Fowlis Wester car park
Refreshments:	None
Ordnance Survey maps:	Rangefinder 58 (Perth & Kinross), Pathfinder 349 NN 82/92 (Crieff)

General description *This is a far more interesting and varied walk than might appear from a glance at the map, taking in a charming village with a history, standing stones, moorland, woodland and, above all, sweeping views over Strathearn to the Ochils. Most of the way provides easy going on good tracks or country lanes, but there are one or two places which can be wet and muddy.*

*As this walk includes passing through a farmyard and crossing pastures with pet sheep and other animals, as well as a grouse moor, dogs must be kept on the lead. Also note that the ford across the Muckle Burn at **D** may be at least ankle deep when in spate.*

Fowlis Wester is a ½-mile (0.75 km) north of the A85 and 5 miles (8 km) east of Crieff. Now only a few homes clustered round a small square with paintbox-coloured cottage gardens and hanging baskets on the lampposts, it is picturesque but seemingly unimportant. It may be today, but it once stood on the main road to Perth along which Highlanders drove their cattle. Its cattle market was as important as that at Falkirk. The Parish Church of St Bean or Beanus dates from the thirteenth century, and the parish encompasses most of the now depopulated uplands between Glen Almond and Strathearn and a large area of the strath itself. A look inside the church can be left to the end of the walk, which starts at the Pictish stone in the village square. This is a replica of the one which stood there for centuries but was moved inside the church in 1991 to preserve it.

From the square and facing the church, turn left up a little lane in front of a large white house and continue on to a farm road **(A)** passing through arable fields. Turn up right at the sign to Crofthead **(B)**, walk across the farmyard and through a metal gate into a pasture with cows and sheep. Be prepared to be mobbed by the sheep which are all farm pets. At the far left corner of this field, on the other side of a rickety fence, is a solitary standing stone with another recumbent one nearby. To reach the stone it is necessary to climb the fence and jump a deep ditch, but it can be well inspected without doing that.

Continue on alongside the fence to the right to a hurdle, climb over it and keep alongside the wall to another metal gate, on the other side of which is a grass road running west along a contour of the hillside. On your left the patchwork fields of Strathearn lie flat all the way to the Ochils, showing as a line of gentle downs the length of the horizon. In the immediate foreground the field pattern is broken by the extensive woods of the great estate of Abercairney, which once

The shop-cum-post office at the start of the walk in Fowlis Wester, once a drovers' market town

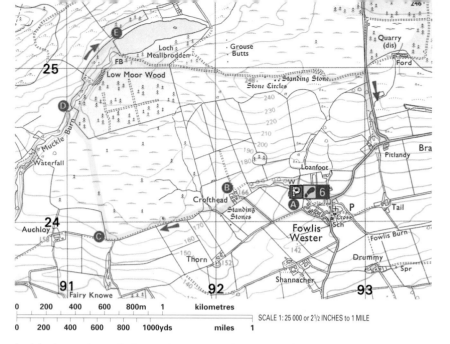

had the largest house in Perthshire, a neo-Gothic building now demolished and replaced by a modern house. This is a most pleasant path bordered by wild flowers and, rising gently to the right, purple heather moorland studded with innumerable bleached tree-stumps of a long-vanished forest.

After a time this path comes to the gate to Auchloy, at which point a coarse stone forestry road (C) – not shown on the map – heads north towards Low Moor Wood. Before walking up this road, pause to take in the view up the strath to Crieff which peeps out from beside the Knock of Crieff, making it seem swaddled in trees. Arriving at the corner of Low Moor Wood, which is well fenced, the road zigzags along its boundary and heads down the steep slope of the gorge through which runs Muckle Burn and then crosses a ford (D) which will be at least ankle deep when the burn is in spate.

Immediately after crossing the burn and going through a gate, climb a short, steep grass slope to the right and keep walking parallel to the wood's wire fence, which is mostly buried in shoulder-high ferns. On the way, a collapsed iron gate has to be climbed over, after which there are intermittent views through the trees of the little loch ahead. The way, which is not a path but shows signs of having been trodden before, dips downhill and becomes wet underfoot. Where the fence takes a sharp right turn, just before the loch, climb over a stile (E) into the wood, walk back a few yards and then go over the grass-topped embankment across the

foot of the loch. On the other side is a footbridge across the overspill into Muckle Burn, and then a path heads up into the wood past a boathouse.

This woodland path climbs gently up under tall conifers with a tufted floor of sphagnum moss and other wetland plants. Emerging from the wood through a metal gate, the path becomes a rough road which crosses a grouse moor to the Fowlis Wester–Buchanty road. On the way one gets a close look at the construction of some grouse butts, somewhat reminiscent of pictures of World War I dugouts. Beside the road is a fine upstanding stone and several others lying down which once formed a circle. Of a late summer's evening the moor is vibrant with the purple of the heather and the varied greens of grass, ferns and distant pines. After a clear day the low evening light perfectly illuminates the fields and copses of Strathearn, bringing the Ochils into closer focus. It is a truly panoramic walk.

The moorland road ends at a set of double gates leading onto the motor road, where you turn right to return to Fowlis Wester. It is downhill all the way, facing the lovely view over Strathearn. The last change in direction is at the Pitlandy T-junction, where one turns right downhill. Now the church should be visited to see the leper window, the original Pictish stone and another which was found imbedded in the wall during restoration work in 1927. The village has a small shop-cum-post office, and it is pleasant to see it still has a red telephone-box. □

7 Allean Forest, Tay Forest Park

Start: Queen's View Visitor Centre, Loch Tummel

Distance: 4½ miles (7.25 km)

Approximate time: 2½ hours

Parking: Queen's View Visitor Centre

Refreshments: None

Ordnance Survey maps: Landrangers 52 (Pitlochry & Aberfeldy) and 43 (Braemar), Pathfinders 294 NN 86/96 (Blair Atholl & Killiecrankie) and 309 NN 85/95 (Pitlochry)

General description Forestry tracks through massed ranks of bare pine trunks can be a bit monotonous unless there are other things to see and views to be reached. Allean Forest near the foot of Loch Tummel has plenty of both: a waterside walk, splendid views of loch and mountain, an eighteenth-century clachan and an eighth-century ring fort, also a neolithic standing stone, although this is off the beaten track. There is a varied mix of conifers on the high ground and broadleaf trees near the loch, while the terrain gives some good walking with

several expectations of surprise views. For those wishing to learn as well as walk, the history, development and management of the whole Tay Forest Park is explained by graphics and audio-visual displays at the visitor centre.

The visitor centre is 3 miles (4.75 km) along the B8019 Kinloch Rannoch road after crossing Garry Bridge. A signposted path leads from it to Queen's View **(A)** above Loch Tummel, where Queen Victoria picnicked with John Brown in 1866. It is one of the classic views, reproduced on a million postcards. From a height of 700 feet (213 m) the view takes in the whole length of the loch with its wooded islets and hillsides all the way to Buachaille Etive above Glencoe. In the near distance is the distinctive summit of Schiehallion, one of the shapeliest of mountains. From Queen's View, take the narrow path which starts parallel with the road **(B)** and then dives down through mixed conifers and broadleafs to the lochside. White posts keep you on the right track, and plaques describe the surrounding woodland habitat. After running a short distance along the lochside, the path climbs back up to a point on the road opposite the entrance **(C)** to Allean Forest car park and picnic site. Walk up the forest road which curves to the left, passing a gap in the trees which offers a vista down the loch almost as good as the Queen's View.

Ignoring a track off to the right (at point **G**, you will return here later), keep on

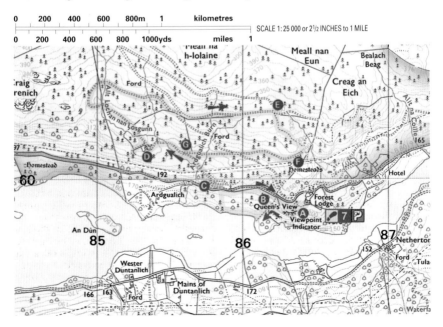

28

The famous Queen's view at the foot of Loch Tummel. Schiehallion rises on the far horizon

uphill until reaching the site of a restored eighteenth-century clachan **(D)** of three houses, a byre, wool-dyeing shed and kiln. The main building is turf-roofed, and one can go in through a low doorway to look at the interior, which is much like that of the black houses lived in by crofters all over the Highlands for centuries. It has an open hearth in the middle of the floor and a fire-pit for a fleece-dyeing cauldron. The other buildings are roofless. From here a short path leads to yet another viewpoint overlooking Loch Tummel. Back on the forest road, climb steadily to the summit of the walk at 1,280 feet (390 m), crossing on the way Allt Lochan nan Losguin, a long name for a small burn that tumbles through the undergrowth. Beside the road, trees have seeded themselves and grown to bonzai-like replicas of their elders, and the ditches are home to a variety of bog plants and mosses. In the forestry, Douglas firs have been planted on the rocky ground, pines amongst the heather, spruces in the grassy areas and larches where there is bracken. This is the habitat of the goldcrest, coal-tit, crossbill, siskin and lesser redpoll. Buzzards and sparrow-hawks nest about 30 feet (9 m) above the ground in larch-trees and, come spring, black grouse will be heard hissing and making a lot of disturbance during courtship and mating.

The rest of the walk is downhill but for one short rise in the ground which occurs where a new plantation sloping down to the loch has yet to reach 12 feet (3.5 m),

and so for a few years there will be a good view over the tops to the hills east of Pitlochry and beyond to Strathardle. For a while, the road runs level before turning left and back on itself, but at this point follow the arrow pointing right on a red post **(E)**. This directs you onto a grass path which winds downhill between trees whose overhanging branches make all dark and silent and heavy with the scent of pine, which one does not get on the broad forest roads. Suddenly there is a jump down a small bank onto another forest road where another red post points to the right. In a few moments one sees a pile of stones in a clearing off the road **(F)**. On the map they are called homesteads, but they turn out to be the remains of an eighth-century ring fort whose walls of heavy boulders stand about 4 feet (1.2 m) high and are 10 feet (3 m) thick. There are entrances on both the east and west sides of the circle which are aligned with a clearing through the forestry, giving a view down to Loch Tummel. The fort has a diameter of 78 feet (23 m).

From here the walk continues straight on down through Scots pines to meet the forest road **(G)** coming up from the car park and picnic site. It is then a ½-mile (0.75 km) up the B8019 back to the visitor centre, but it is more pleasant and safer from holiday traffic to cross over the road and go along the upper leg of the lochside circular walk which runs through the woods parallel with the road. □

8 Cloan Glen

Start:	Auchterarder
Distance:	5 miles (8 km)
Approximate time:	2½ hours
Parking:	Pottery car park, Auchterarder
Refreshments:	Hotels, restaurant, pubs and café in Auchterarder
Ordnance Survey maps:	Landranger 58 (Perth & Kinross), Pathfinder 360 NN 81/91 (Auchterarder & Muthill)

General description *This easy and pleasant country walk through a private glen with views of the nearby Ochil Hills and the more distant Grampians starts in a small town noted for its antique shops. The days of the family butcher are not over in Auchterarder, where there are two which would not be out of place in the heart of London's Mayfair. The start of the walk is conveniently just off the A9 road to Perth and Inverness and about 2 miles (3.25 km) from the famous Gleneagles Hotel.*

Note that there is pheasant-shooting in the woods surrounding Cloan Glen on five Saturdays in winter, so from November to February it is imperative that walkers stick to the glen road and do not wander off up any of the footpaths among the trees. The public will only remain welcome in Cloan Glen so long as they do no damage, leave no litter and keep their dogs on the leash.

Auchterarder, which is strung along a 1-mile (1.5 km) main street, was the head burgh in the Earldom of Strathearn before becoming a royal burgh. It was burned down in 1715 by the Jacobite Earl of Mar, so most of what is seen today is, historically, quite modern. The Free Church of Scotland was founded here in the mid-nineteenth century. As might be expected of a town near Gleneagles Hotel, it has some excellent shops.

The walk must be started from the edge of the town as the lanes leading to the glen are too narrow and winding for roadside parking. Walkers are welcome to use the John Maguire Pottery car park at the bottom of Abbey Road, which is near the east end of the long High Street. From there, walk over the Ruthven Water bridge and then the bridge over the A9 and follow the lane as it turns right, then

curves to the left and passes under the railway line (**A**). From this point on one is looking towards the foothills of the Ochils. Most prominent is the 1,344-foot (410 m) lump of Craig Rossie (the subject of Walk 11), looking very dominant where it is although only a big hill compared with the mountains of the Highlands, which start not many miles to the north.

Tucked into the wooded hillside straight ahead are the towers and battlements of Cloan, a country-house masquerading as a Scottish baronial castle in the Victorian Gothic style. It marks the start of Cloan Glen, which is part of its 3,500-acre (1,416 ha) woodland estate. In walking along the lane towards the house you will be walking in the carriage tracks, if not the footsteps, of many famous men, for it is the seat of the Haldane family. Here Lord Haldane of Cloan, War Minister and then Lord Chancellor, entertained the good and the great during the first quarter of this century. The visitors' book is inscribed by generals Haig and Roberts of World War I, by Asquith and Earl Grey, James Barry, an archbishop of Canterbury, John Buchan, and Sidney and Beatrice Webb, among a marvellous mixture of writers, politicians, soldiers and clergy. It is something to be thinking about as you approach the house, which is private. Just before the entrance to the drive (**B**), there is a notice at the foot of Cloan Glen which asks you to keep your dog on a lead and forbids horses, bicycles and cars, although the present owner, Mr Richard Haldane, welcomes walkers.

In early summer there is a splurge of bright colour from rhododendrons which have strayed from the big garden above. The path soon comes alongside the Cloan Burn, where there is a building (**C**) half-hidden among the trees and undergrowth, which contained a water-driven sawmill and turbine to produce electricity for the house. The turbine was superseded by the national grid only in 1952. Water for the sawmill is still fed by pipes from higher up the glen, and they also feed the fire-hydrants and fountains in the garden. A few minutes' walk further up the glen one spies another building, now roofless, which the Haldane children call the Witch's House; it also once housed a turbine which was fed by a mile-long leat, traces of which are difficult to find.

The glen is largely planted with Douglas fir and grand fir, but there is also an abundant quantity of oak, ash, alder, sycamore, beech, birch and rowan as well as wild cherry and chestnut to make for variety, interest and pleasant colour.

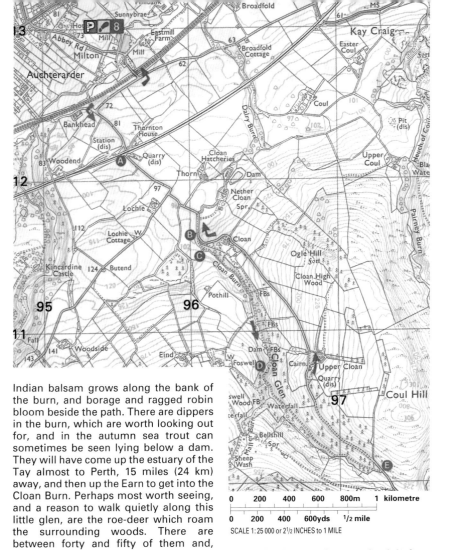

Indian balsam grows along the bank of the burn, and borage and ragged robin bloom beside the path. There are dippers in the burn, which are worth looking out for, and in the autumn sea trout can sometimes be seen lying below a dam. They will have come up the estuary of the Tay almost to Perth, 15 miles (24 km) away, and then up the Earn to get into the Cloan Burn. Perhaps most worth seeing, and a reason to walk quietly along this little glen, are the roe-deer which roam the surrounding woods. There are between forty and fifty of them and, because they are never shot at, they are less timid than most.

At one point the burn takes a double bend (D) across the path and has to be forded. But if hopping from stone to stone is not your forte, there is a narrow track which goes up and then down through the trees to a footbridge to put you on the path again dry-shod. After the fords the going becomes a little steeper, and the path veers away from the water from a point where it becomes quite tumbled and there is the sound of water falling. In fact, two waterfalls can be heard but not easily seen when all the trees are in leaf. The falls are named Connell's Spout after a man who was said to have had an illicit still in a cave behind them.

Eventually, after passing a stretch brilliant with gorse, the path reaches a gate (E) at the top of the glen and comes out onto the lane which has come up from

SCALE 1:25 000 or 2¹/₂ INCHES to 1 MILE

Cloan. The lane continues to the right for a few hundred yards to Coulshill Farm and then becomes a track across moorland, leading to Glen Devon and thence to Glen Eagles. Turn left on the lane back down to Cloan and the point where you entered the glen. Serving only a couple of houses and a farm, there will be little or no traffic on the lane, which is lined with oaks. After a while the trees of the glen drop well below eye-level, and one is afforded a clear line of sight over their tops to the western Grampians. Ben Vorlich, 3,231 feet (985 m), is prominent straight ahead, and slightly to its right and further off is Ben Lawers, at 3,984 feet (1,214 m) the highest mountain in Perthshire. Most of the way back to the gateway to Cloan is downhill, and then it is a matter of retracing your steps back to the town, the whole of which can be clearly seen from the hillside. □

9 Rannoch Forest

Start:	Carie by Loch Rannoch
Distance:	6½ miles (10.5 km)
Approximate time:	3½ hours
Parking:	Forest car park, Carie
Refreshments:	None
Ordnance Survey maps:	Landranger 51 (Loch Tay), Pathfinders 308 NN 65/75 (Kinloch Rannoch & Schiehallion) and 307 NN 45/55 (Loch Rannoch (West))

General description The Forestry Commission have an open access policy, but they do not publicise all the many walks through their forests. The Black Wood of Rannock on the southern shore of Loch Rannoch is the last remnant of the ancient Caledonian Forest which covered much of Scotland after the last Ice Age 11,000 years ago. Predominantly Scots pine and birch but also some willow, alder and rowan with a dense mat of mosses, it is both a beautiful woodland and a fragile one. Consequently it is one in which they would prefer not to have walkers. From Carie up the Allt na Bogair glen above a deep gorge and then back by a right-of-way to Dall along the loch shore, this charming walk passes through a stand of Caledonian pines, descendants of the ancient woodland, and ends beside the Black Wood of Rannoch. These woods support a wide variety of birds and wildlife, including red squirrels, pine martens, wildcats and capercaillie.

If in search of more local knowledge, walk over the footbridge in the corner of the car park and up the path to Kilvrecht Campsite in the hope that the warden is in his office. It would be productive to have a chat with him before starting the walk.

Rannoch School beside the ancient Black Wood

Follow the road along the south bank of Loch Rannoch from Kinloch Rannoch for about 3 miles (4.75 km) and turn off at the second Forestry Commission parking and picnic sign, unless looking for a campsite, in which case take the first forest road to Kilvrecht Campsite. They are adjacent. In the car park, walk over to the far left corner to a footbridge over the Allt na Bogair **(A)** to look at the falling water being driven through a narrow rock venturi beneath it. The scouring effect of the water has carved a smooth scoop out of the opposing rockface, as a spoon does cutting through the flesh of an avocado pear.

Walk across the neighbouring picnic site to a signpost bearing a white footprint. Follow this along the forest track, which slowly rises through the trees above the floor of the glen. This is a natural woodland of Scots pine, birch and rowan, completely filling the gorge below and hiding the burn from view. Still higher along the track is managed forestry of Scots and lodgepole pine, Sitka spruce, larch and birch. There is a rich ground cover of mosses with several types of sphagnum, together with an abundance of wild flowers in season – lesser celandine, wood sorrel and anemone and, not least, primrose – and everywhere a great variety of fungi and lichens. The botanically minded walker will not hurry by. Near the start of the climb up the glen there is a crag and detached boulder about the size of a small house **(B)** lying beside the track to provide a bit of fun for those who like a scramble. The top of the boulder affords a good view up and down the glen. At about the highest point on the path, just over 1,000 feet (305 m) above sea-level, a flat piece of ground in a break in the trees forms a vertiginous platform for viewing **(C)** down onto the treetops and up the sheer tree-covered rockface of the opposite side of the gorge. It is a sight to make one wonder just how trees can take root on a vertical rockface and grow strong and vertical too. But they do in all the best glens.

Eventually the track heads downhill, and the trees below thin out to show the burn emerging from its rocky gorge and flowing along a flat, marshy valley floor. Where the track meets the water there is a footbridge leading to a small path which goes back on the other side of the glen. Just before this bridge is the stand of Scots pines, an extension of those in the nearby Black Wood. Ignore the short path leading to the bridge and bear right, following a sign **(D)** to Glen Lyon, to come out onto a broad and hard-packed stone forestry road. Turn right down this road past an irregular-shaped lochan among the trees. Soon there appears to be a T-junction ahead. Actually it is the road turning left; the apparent right-hand arm is no more than 15 yards (14 m) long.

Do not take the left-hand bend, but walk straight ahead and enter the forestry by a narrow footpath (E) almost hidden among the trees. It runs downhill all the way to Dall, where a new and colourful life has been given to an old country-house with more than a passing resemblance to Blair Castle. Now Rannoch School, this establishment is less orthodox than most schools, with an ethos loosely based on the ideal of Kurt Hahn, founder of Gordonstoun. The narrow path down to Dall varies from an easy earth surface to some rocky, rutted patches and one boggy section. On the way it emerges onto another broad forestry road but quickly dives back into the trees on the other side. Continuing through a mix of conifer and broadleaf, one soon comes out onto level ground behind the school where its sailing dinghies are parked. Take the road which goes off to the right skirting the school playing-fields and golf-course to meet the lochside road by a red telephone-box. On this penultimate leg of the walk one may, during term-time, see some of the multifarious outdoor activities of the school in progress.

One can either turn right up the road for the 1½-mile (2.5 km) walk back to Carie and the Forestry Commission car park or, more pleasantly, walk most of the way along the boulder-strewn foreshore of the loch, while contemplating the waters which produce some of the biggest brown trout in Scotland. ☐

SCALE 1:25 000 or 2½ INCHES to 1 MILE

10 Birks of Aberfeldy

Start:	Birks signpost beside Crieff road, Aberfeldy
Distance:	4 miles (6.5 km)
Approximate time:	2½ hours
Parking:	Birks of Aberfeldy car park, Crieff road
Refreshments:	Hotels, pubs and café in Aberfeldy
Ordnance Survey maps:	Rangefinder 52 (Pitlochry & Aberfeldy), Pathfinder 323 NN 84/94 (Aberfeldy)

General description *This is an extension of a popular 200-year-old walk through the steep, wooded gorge of the Moness Den with its sheer rockfaces and noisy waterfalls. The extension takes in wide, high-level views over Strath Tay and the town of Aberfeldy. The paths along the edges of rock precipices have been made easier and safer with hand-rails and walkways bridging awkward places. However, it is still quite a steep walk, ascending some 600 feet (183 m) in a mile (1.5 km). The Birks of Aberfeldy are the subject of a Burns poem of the same name.*

Soon after the footpath leaves the car park at the foot of the glen it splits into two. Take the left fork **(A)** over a footbridge above a small waterfall. After a stand of beech-trees, the path starts climbing through the natural woodland of the glen, a mix of wych-elm, ash and willow, rowan, guelder rose, oak and hazel. Ferns of many varieties are prolific. Wintergreen and wood vetch prosper in the wet ground and flower from June to August. The Moness Burn is chock-a-block with huge boulders, many of which must weigh two or three tons. The glen was formed by the gouging action of the retreating glaciers about 10,000 years ago, and the numerous waterfalls are formed by streams tumbling down the side of the glen and by the main burn flowing over bands of hard rock. However hard rock is, it will, little by little, be eroded by the action of water, especially when it freezes in a fissure, expands and cracks the rock. Chunks fall off and clutter the floor of the valley.

The wee burns falling down the rockside have been bridged, making the going easier and drier, but they provide pretty sights, especially where steps and bridges take the path higher in a spiral staircase configuration round the falling water. Nearing the top of the glen, the path follows a hairpin bend **(B)** to climb suddenly much higher, but there is another path which keeps straight ahead

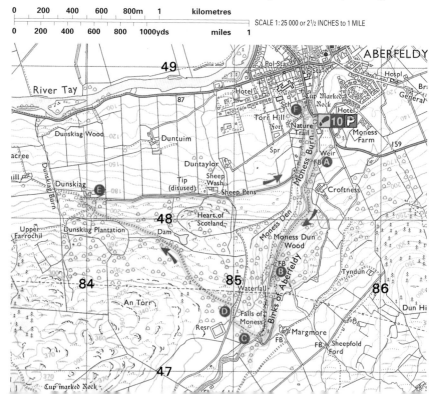

0	200	400	600	800m	1	kilometres
0	200	400	600	800	1000yds	miles 1

SCALE 1: 25 000 or 2½ INCHES to 1 MILE

There are expansive views up and down Strath Tay from the summit of this walk

for a few yards to a fenced, rock platform overlooking a flight of five cascades, each falling into a pill. Take the hairpin bend. The path goes by steps and bridges to the top edge of the glen, where the trees give way to fields. Ahead now, well below the path, are the Falls of Moness, dropping 80 feet (24 m) over a stone sill. Continue along the path and then go up onto the opposite flank of the glen where there is a closer view from a bridge spanning the top of the falls. From here there is a straightforward, unspectacular forest path leading downhill back to the car park.

Ignore this route back. At the top of the short slope up from the bridge, turn off left onto a narrow footpath (C), little more than a rabbit-run, which takes you uphill a bit through a broadleaf-wood and onto the farm road from Urlar. Turn right on this road and go downhill about 100 yards (91 m) and through a gate on the left (D). You are then on another farm road, mostly grass, and little used by its appearance. This descends gently through thinly spaced trees for nearly a mile (1.5 km) to Dunskiag (E), a fairly large farmhouse with outbuildings, all empty and forlorn on the hillside overlooking the River Tay. The farm road from Farrochill to the west passes Dunskiag and takes you all the way back into Aberfeldy. It is a road with uninterrupted views to the north and provides plenty to look at. The tip of Ben Lawers can be glimpsed to the west and, panning a little to its right, one sees the top of Schiehallion. Immediately across the strath is Castle Menzies, a sixteenth-century fortified tower-house now in the care of the clan society and open to the public. Next to it is seen the tiny village of Weem with The Weem, a whitewashed old inn, clearly visible. It was there that General Wade lodged while building his military roads and bridges hereabouts. There is a portrait of him on the outside wall. There is no public bar, only a cocktail bar for residents and those using the restaurant. However, it may be possible for walkers to be served sitting outside in summer.

Aberfeldy is seen complete in the embrace of a curve of the Tay, which is crossed by Wade's bridge built in 1733 to a design by William Adam, father of Robert Adam, Scotland's most famous architect. It was the most ambitious of thirty-five major bridges along a network of 250 miles (402 km) of new roads and the only one still surviving as a functioning highway. There is a strange obelisk at all four corners of the centre arch, and the stone parapet is so high that it cannot be looked over. Its strategic importance in Scotland's first proper road system is obvious to see from the high level of the farm road. To the right of Wade's bridge, on the edge of the golf-course, is a white pedestrian suspension bridge – the first in the world to be constructed of glass fibre.

The farm road drops down into the outskirts of the town to become a street, ending at the junction with Crieff Road (F), the A826, running south from the town centre. Turn right at this junction. The car park is then 200 yards (183 m) on the right. Incidentally, water from the Moness Burn flows for 500 yards (457 m) from the bottom of the glen through a tunnel under the houses to power a water mill. □

11 Craig Rossie

Start:	Pairney Farm
Distance:	3¾ miles (6 km)
Approximate time:	2½ hours
Parking:	Pairney Farm
Refreshments:	Hotels, restaurant, pubs and café in Auchterarder
Ordnance Survey maps:	Landranger 58 (Perth & Kinross), Pathfinder 360 NN 81/91 (Auchterarder & Muthill)

General description Craig Rossie is the first hill of any character which one sees when entering Perthshire along the A9, a few minutes' drive out of Auchterarder, and is a more energetic alternative to the Cloan Glen walk alongside it. It makes a good practice hill for bigger ones to come. For its modest height of 1,345 feet (410 m) the views from the top are quite extensive, taking in Ben Lomond to the west and the Tay estuary and Dundee to the east. At its feet is the chequer-board field pattern of Strathearn and, of course, Auchterarder and the Gleneagles Hotel. Craig Rossie is geographically an outpost of the northern slopes of the Ochils, which is certainly why it had a fort on one of its summits. Note that passing the deep bowl of Hologrogin could be dangerous in mist.

Leave the A9 by the B8062 going east and signposted to Dunning. Soon after passing under a railway bridge, park in the yard of Pairney Farm. The owners, Mr and Mrs Mitchell, allow walkers this facility, but you must ask exactly where to

The forestry fence aids walkers coming off Craig Rossie as the way down becomes almost vertical

park (0764 663568) so as not to obstruct farm vehicles. You may be directed to a farm track further up the road.

The walk starts on the rough road (A) at the back of the farm, going south beside Pairney Burn round a large working quarry. There is a sign warning of the danger of falling rocks and telling you to keep away from the quarry face. The remains of a fort are not worth looking at, so keep on the road, which is wide enough for lorry traffic, to Green's Burn, which flows under it beside a sweet chestnut-tree. The bulk of Craig Rossie rises steep-to on the left. The road now starts to climb away from Pairney Burn, and ahead on the hillside can be seen Coul, Small, Lee and Beldhill burns which feed it. Curving round behind Beld Hill, the road is joined on the right by a 4-foot-(1.2 m) high fence and continues along-side it for further than is shown on the map. At the point where it starts going down to meet Beldhill Burn, turn onto a deeply rutted vehicle track (B) up the side of Beld Hill, from the top of which the hills beyond Crieff and Comrie can be seen. Here the track forks. Take the left fork (C) and make for Ben Effrey, a big green hill straight ahead. A fort on the top of Ben Effrey had steep, natural defences on three sides, those on the west being precipitous. Access was along the ridge from the 1,190-foot (363 m) spot height, about 328 feet (100 m) south of the fort. This open south flank was defended by two parallel drystone walls about 10 feet (3 m) apart, which have long since crum-bled away. There are slight indications of terracing on the north and east sides of the hill. This is a comfortable picnic spot.

After visiting the site of the fort retrace your steps to the Land-Rover track and follow it over towards the perimeter fence (D) of the forestry at the 1,351-foot (412 m) spot height. Continue north alongside the fence, and soon the quite impressive cliff on the east face of Craig Rossie comes into view. Then the vehicle track peters out, but you are left with a sheep-run to the base of the crag. From the triangulation pillar standing at 1,345 feet (410 m), one looks east over the forestry on Green Hill to Rossie Law, another hill with a fort on its brow. Further east, Dunning is seen lying in flat agricultural land with roads running from it like the spokes of a wheel. The A9 dual carriageway stretches ahead with lots of toy cars and lorries running back and forth, seemingly in an awful hurry. The top of Craig Rossie is a small grass plateau about 200 yards (183 m) east to west, with a small cliff-face to the west

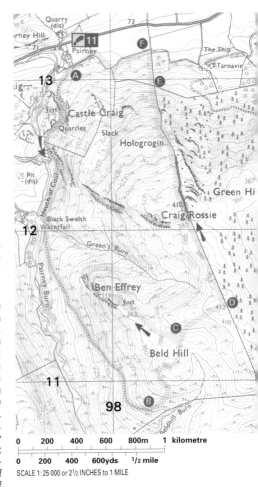

SCALE 1:25 000 or 2½ INCHES to 1 MILE

and sheer, steep cliffs with scree at the bottom to the east. It is easiest to carry on following the fence through tussocky grass and heather, leaving it only to avoid steep, rocky patches. Along this stretch through the fence, out of reach of the sheep, there is in the late summer a feast of blaeberries (bilberries) to be had. Picking them can add quite a bit of time to the walk. Pairney Farm is now in view below, and on the way one passes a deep bowl in the ground, shown as Hologrogin on the map. It might be a hazard to fall into in heavy mist. The fence posts provide handy supports as the path steepens on its final descent to another fence (E), running east to west across it. Climb over this fence and continue down to a drystone wall (F), turning left to keep alongside it to a gate into a field. Once through that, continue hugging the wall to arrive at a last gate onto the quarry road behind the farm from where the walk started. □

12 Castle Dow

Start:	Balnaguard
Distance:	4¼ miles (7 km)
Approximate time:	2½ hours
Parking:	Waste ground by bus-stop, Balnaguard
Refreshments:	None
Ordnance Survey maps:	Landranger 52 (Pitlochry & Aberfeldy), Pathfinder 309 NN 85/95 (Pitlochry)

General description *This is an uphill walk through forestry to a commanding hilltop, the site of a Pictish fort, cup-marked stones, cairns and a hut circle. The views are grand and distant. From point C, the return to a charming little village covers rough and muddy ground through undergrowth, so stout, water-proof footwear and clothing are recommended. This is virtually an undiscovered walk.*

Start in Balnaguard, a charming hamlet with no shape to it, just a clutch of stone cottages set higgledy-piggledy on the hill slope and nestling in pretty gardens wrapped around with stone walls. Walk 1 mile (1.5 km) north-west along the minor road on the south bank of the River Tay, past a campsite at Sketewan, to the start of a forestry road on the left (**A**). This road climbs in a wide sweep, ascending about 800 feet (244 m) to a point 150 feet (46 m) below the hilltop site of Castle Dow. The going is rough but firm, through a mix of natural woodland of Scots pine, yew and birch. On the way there are ever-improving views down the River Tay as it winds through the flat-bottomed valley of light-green fields, beyond which rise steep, forested hills in dark green. Fox-gloves and purple heather in season provide splashes of colour. From the road a newly made-up path (**B**) starts the final climb to Castle Dow, then keep alongside a stone wall to the 1,115-foot (340 m) summit. The eye is held by a row of seven tall cairns lining the edge of the east-facing escarpment. They date only from the nineteenth century but they do make foreground frames for a selection of magnificent views, particularly down Strath Tay. One can look east to the Point of Logierait, Ballinluig and the Tulliemet hills, then west to the Farragon Hills and over Aberfeldy and Weem to the great

Grampian massif marching across the distant horizon, with the ubiquitous cone summit of Shiehallion.

The archaeological sites on this draughty plateau are less prominent. There are a lot of stones about, some half-buried and others piled two or three high, so for serious study an eight-figure grid reference is needed. The fort at NN 9294 5132 consists of a boulder-faced, rubble wall. Originally about 10 feet (3 m) thick, it has disappeared along the top of the steep cliff on the east side. An ante-chamber is attached to the south-west corner. There are traces of further defences, such as a grass-covered stone rampart and a ditch, but if there were any internal walls there is no sign of them. The most obvious structure is a sheepfold, obviously made from stones taken from the fort. Downhill in a north-westerly direction at NN 9254 5162 are the slight remnants of a circular stone hut with walls 5 feet (1.5 m) thick. Nearby is a stone set up on edge with other broken ones lying around, while on a ridge to the west the peat-covered remains of a cairn stand some 3 feet (0.9 m) high.

Leaving the fort area, return the way you came to the forestry road and walk down it as far as an open gateway on the second bend (**C**). Here the road can be left for a shorter and more adventurous return to the village. Less adventurous walkers may wish to retrace their steps to the start. The right-hand gatepost is at the very corner of a recent plantation with a neat wire fence running downhill along its north boundary. Turn sharp right through the gateway and follow the fence along long grass, avoiding as much as possible the patches of reeds where the ground is squidgy. Also take it slowly because there are lots of little mounds and hollows hidden underfoot. There is no path at all so this is rough-going, but it does not last long.

On the way there is one rather decayed two-bar wooden fence to duck under or step over. After about ten minutes pushing through the high grass a small unnamed burn crosses one's path from the plantation. Turn left and keep it company over open ground, but a little above it to find firm footing. Eventually it flows under another fence, at which point walk uphill beside that fence to a stile (**D**). Cross over onto steeply sloping moorland and move down the slope, edging slightly to the left until, over the false horizon, a line of wizened juniper trees can be seen. Make for them and follow them down to a run-off which is more mud than water. Select the easiest place to cross over to

Strange cairns on the summit of Castle Dow with its Pictish fort and views of the Grampian massif

dry ground, but whatever you do your shoes will be covered in mud. The junipers are now thick on the ground, and finding a way between them can be a prickly business. They are leftovers from the time when Scotland had a thriving export trade in juniper berries to Holland as the flavouring ingredient in gin-distilling. They were also a panacea for many ills in the Highlands, and burning juniper bushes was the accepted form of fumigating in cases of infectious disease.

A rough, stony and muddy path leads through the trees to a stone wall, at which it bears right towards the village. At a stile beside a notice saying that you have just come through Balnaguard Glen Wildlife Reserve, cross over and take a grass road down to a gateway behind a new bungalow into Balnaguard. □

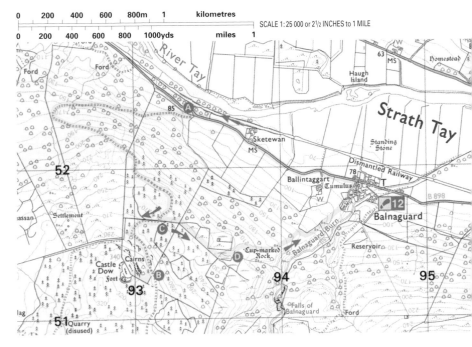

13 Chapel Stone to Meall a' Charra

Start:	Chapel Stone, Wester Clunie
Distance:	5 miles (8 km)
Approximate time:	2½ hours
Parking:	Layby near Chapel Stone
Refreshments:	Hotels, restaurants, pubs and cafés in Pitlochry
Ordnance Survey maps:	Landranger 52 (Pitlochry & Aberfeldy), Pathfinder 309 NN 85/95 (Pitlochry)

General description *This is a walk for those who like to have the world to themselves for a while and relish a little steep rough walking, finding their own way with only a hilltop ahead to guide them. The going will probably be wet in places, and the 2,023-foot (617 m) summit is exposed. The views on the way and at the top are as good as many found on better-known and well-trodden routes.*

The Chapel Stone, which marks the start of this walk, stands on a bank beside the road which runs along the south bank of Loch Faskally. This quiet minor road begins as a turn-off from the section of the new A9, where it bypasses Pitlochry and is signposted to Wester Clunie.

Although not much to look at, the stone, about 4 feet (1.2 m) high with a cross of primitive appearance incised on its face, dates back to the seventh century and is the oldest ecclesiastical relic in the district. About 50 yards (46 m) from the stone there is an unmarked layby, recognisable by a white concrete waste bin. Next to it, a gate leads into a sloping field of long grass. Walk up this slope for a few yards to come onto an old cart-track well overgrown, and then follow it to the left. At first it rises gently and then more steeply through an area of shoulder-high ferns. These have to be pushed aside to reveal the track, so clothing will get wet after rain. After a bit of a zigzag, the track sweeps round in a right-hand curve to come out on an almost flat plateau below Dùn Beag, 'small fort'. There is no sign of a fort, only the ruins of a farmstead **(A)**, from where one gets a nice view of Loch Faskally and Pitlochry, backed by the great turreted bulk of the Royal Atholl Hotel. The hotel was built when the railway arrived, ensuring that the town attracted the best type of tourist.

The track now changes direction to climb westward under a power-line before passing through a stand of birch.

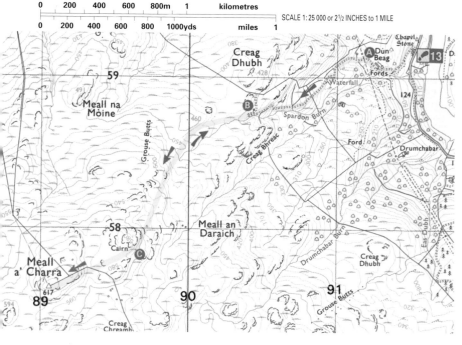

The seventh-century Chapel Stone marks the start of the walk up to the remote Meall a' Charra

After quite a bit of twisting about, the path clears the trees and reaches a more barren terrain of heather, with the high lump of Creag Dhubh to one side and the escarpment of Creag Bhreac on the other. Then it turns sharp right and suddenly stops just beyond a ruined hut **(B)**. Should you continue, the path leads onto boggy ground beside the Spardon Burn and then onto some slippery, sloping rock slabs. To avoid this, go the few yards to the hut and plot a course between the burn and spot height 460, where the ground is firmer. There is a track of sorts through the heather, almost certainly a rabbit-run, but it soon peters out, and a way must be found across open moorland. Aim for the squat cairn **(C)** clearly seen atop a hill 3/4 mile (1.25 km) straight ahead. Choose your own course as the ground allows and make for a slight saddle on the left of the cairn for the approach to the top of the hill. On this leg one first loses a little height and then has a stiff walk up to the cairn from where the destination, Meall a' Charra, is clear, 600 yards (548 m) ahead. Again the way dips, and then there is a final steep section to the top at 2,023 feet (617 m). Despite the fence shown on the map, there are no obstacles on the way to the summit, which is a small plateau with a triangulation pillar.

But why go up to this particular summit? Because on a good day you can see for miles around and be absolutely alone, whereas if you climb the well-signposted and only slightly higher Ben Vrackie on the opposite side of Loch Faskally there could be a lot of people accompanying you up the worn path. Unlike Ben Vrackie, Meall a' Charra does not have a viewpoint indicator, although the views are about as good, so you must read your map to know what you are looking at. You will be looking over Loch Tummel to the north-west and up the Vale of Atholl to the hills of the Forest of Atholl, dominated by Beinn Dearg, 3,307 feet (1,008 m). A pan eastwards takes in Ben Vrackie with its ring of associated summits and beyond them the Beinn a' Ghlo range. If you are in luck, the sun will be shining on the cluster of famous little fishing lochs to the south, the most distinctive being the two Pitcastle lochs. In the west are the Farragon Hills, where they are now mining bauxite. The way back is the same as the way up. ☐

14 Bishop Hill, Kinross

Start:	Scotlandwell
Distance:	5 miles (8 km)
Approximate time:	3 hours
Parking:	Scotlandwell, by church
Refreshments:	Hotels and pubs in Kinnesswood and Scotlandwell
Ordnance Survey maps:	Landranger 58 (Perth & Kinross), Pathfinder 372 NO 00/10 (Kinross)

General description Bishop Hill is on the edge of a high plateau which runs down from West Lomond to overlook the flat plain of the old County of Kinross, now incorporated into Perthshire. It provides a walk of modest length with a short, sharp ascent of about 1,000 feet (305 m) in less than a mile (1.5 km). The views from the top cover a markedly different part of the country to those seen from hills deep in Perthshire, particularly towards Fife and across the Firth of Forth to Edinburgh. Along the top it is easy walking on open,

Carlin Maggie – a witch turned into basalt

soft grassland, and some disused limestone quarries are a fruitful source of fossils. To complete a circular walk it is, unfortunately, necessary to include over a mile along a B-road, but it does have a pavement.

On this walk dogs should be kept on the lead, and watch out for the possibility of a bull at **E** before being confronted!

To reach the walk from Kinross take the A922 out of the town to Milnathort and there turn east onto the B911 to Scotlandwell. Park in the Portmoak church car park on the right side of the road just before coming to Scotlandwell, provided there is no service taking place. If there is, use a layby with space for two or three cars opposite the community centre a little before the church. Should there be no room, go on to Scotlandwell and walk back. To find out times of services telephone 0577 863461. The path to Bishop Hill is signposted about 200 yards (183 m) from the church on the opposite side of the road. A notice requests people to keep dogs on the leash, to fasten gates, to take litter home and not to light fires.

A flight of steps leads to a stile which has to be climbed. Continue on to a wooden bench, from where there is a pleasant view over to Loch Leven. Keep going up through Kilmagad Wood to a narrow corner where the trees end beside a drystone wall. Cross it by another stile **(A)**. There is now a stiff climb on a grass path alongside the wall, which bends to the right, passing beside the spot height of 1,495 feet (456 m) which marks the summit of Munduff Hill. The east side of the wall has recently been planted with saplings. From here, Glenrothes and Fife, and even some oil rigs in the Forth estuary, can be seen to the east, while straight ahead the Lomond Hills, particularly West Lomond's well-rounded top, dominate the north. Munduff's top is a flat plateau with some bumps. Half-left, the highest point on Bishop Hill is the cairn at 1,512 feet (461 m) by the disused quarry, and that is the point to aim for. Going straight there would involve crossing soggy ground in the intervening hollow, so it is better to keep alongside the wall and then go over a stile **(B)** beside a gate onto a well-defined track to the left which – at the time of writing – passes a derelict caravan.

This track leads to two disused quarries on the edge of the escarpment. Looking down from the first one, a great jagged scar of a road cut into the side of the hill winds down towards Easter Balgedie; it

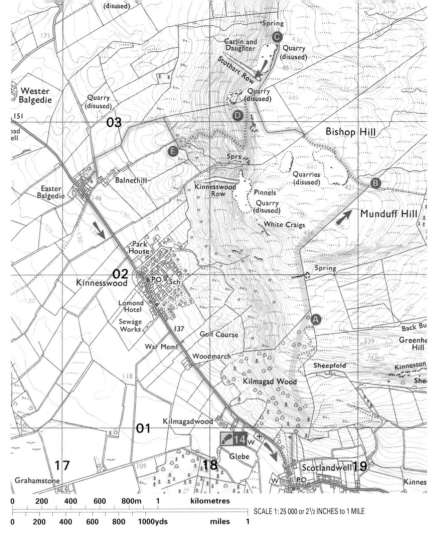

Scale: 0 200 400 600 800m 1 kilometres / 0 200 400 600 800 1000yds miles 1

SCALE 1: 25 000 or 2½ INCHES to 1 MILE

quite spoils the landscape. Continue past this first quarry through a gate in the remains of a stone wall up to the second quarry by the cairn. Both are disused limestone workings which have always been a rich source of fossils and, although plundered over the years, it is still possible to find interesting specimens. Just over the crest of the hill stands a famous landmark, Carlin Maggie, called Carlin and Daughter on the map; the Daughter is further down the hillside. Carlin Maggie is a 40-foot- (12 m) high basalt column, reminiscent of the Old Man of Hoy on the Isle of Skye, with a number of small boulders precariously perched on its top. Legend has it that Maggie was a witch who had a power-struggle with the devil who, striking her with a bolt of lightning, turned her to stone, and there she still stands, forever looking out over Kinross. A gate **(C)** gives access to a good vantage point from which to get a close look at her.

Retrace your steps to above the lower quarry, from where the return leg of the walk starts at the track **(D)** down to Easter Balgedie, except that it does not go the whole way. Steep and sandy and possibly a bit slippery, it is just about suitable for a four-wheel drive vehicle in its lowest gear, but certainly it was never used by quarry trucks. They were not needed as the limestone was just dropped down the steep slope. The track ends at a field **(E)**, across which there are distinct wheel-marks leading to a gate at the far end into the yard of Balnethill, and so into the hamlet of Easter Balgedie. There is sometimes a bull in this field, in which case it would be wiser to turn right at the track end, go through a wooden gate into the adjoining field and walk around the perimeter to Easter Balgedie. Finally there is about a 1-mile (1.5 km) walk along the busy road back to the car park outside Scotlandwell. ☐

15 Den and Hill of Alyth

Start:	Alyth
Distance:	6½ miles (10.5 km)
Approximate time:	3 hours
Parking:	Den of Alyth car park
Refreshments:	Hotels, pubs and cafés in Alyth
Ordnance Survey maps:	Landranger 53 (Blairgowrie), Pathfinders 325 NO 24/34 (Alyth and Glamis) and 311 NO 25/35 (Kirriemuir)

General description *This is an un-demanding walk at the eastern extremity of Perthshire through a deep-sided, wooded valley with a mix of broadleaf trees beside a dynamic boulder-strewn burn. It continues over an old drovers' road across the open moorland of Alyth Hill for far-ranging views over the top of the town to the Sidlaw Hills. There is only one short, steep ascent and no rough-going, but the route may be wet and muddy in parts after rain. The Alyth Burn runs out of the Den and through the centre of Alyth, where little bridges connect the riverside streets.*

Take the road signposted for Bamff due west to the outskirts of Alyth and enter the Den of Alyth car park on the left of the road. From here follow a sign to the glen

walk which starts at the end of a picnic site. The path plunges immediately into dense woodland beside the gravelly Alyth Burn, where the sun is shut out by the canopy of overhanging branches and the vertical rockface towering over the far bank. Over aeons its waters have cut deeply through the old red sandstone of the glen which was quarried in the last century to build the town of Alyth.

The valley was originally created by glaciers moving south like giant bull-dozers from the Cairngorm mass. When they receded 10,000 years ago they poured millions of tons of melt-water into the valley, carrying with it rock debris which first scoured out the glen and then settled in what is now the bed of the burn, which swirls and gushes around boulders and rock obstructions. Where it runs shallow and broad, the bottom is strewn with pebbles polished smooth and round. After a few minutes' walking, the glen broadens out and lets in more light, so it is possible to look into the rock pools for dormant trout and, with luck, see a dipper skimming over the surface or even diving and swimming underwater to feed off freshwater shrimps and stonefly nymphs.

Coming to a footbridge **(A)**, the path divides to run up both sides of the burn. To the right there is mostly beech from here on, so cross the bridge to take the more interesting left-hand path through ash, alder, hazel and oak, the descendants of a forest which has been there for thousands of years. Because the steep sides of the glen made the timber difficult to extract, it has survived the woodman's axe. The path rises and falls, sometimes

Alyth Burn trickles through its glen, here seen from the upper footpath through the Den of Alyth

coming alongside the water, at others passing high above it to give pretty views down through the trees to the beech-groves on the opposite bank. Finally it comes to an end by the old-looking Bridge of Tully (**B**), which was actually only built in 1914. Cross it and immediately dive back into the woods at the far, opposite corner. The burn is now on your left, and the path keeps beside it. Duckboards have been laid in places to span wet patches and stop further erosion of the path. At a fork, keep left alongside the water through a grove of beeches, then bear right and follow the path steeply up to the B952 (**C**), coming up from Alyth. Walk along the road for nearly a mile (1.5 km) uphill to a sign pointing left to Cally and Glen Shee, and right (**D**) – your way – to Glenisla. This road runs uphill beside pine-woods but soon comes out onto moorland with a heavily gorse-covered hill on your right, and on the left open countryside dipping down and up to Balduff Hill 3 miles (4.75 km) off. Soon Newton of Bamff farm comes into view, and at the same moment beside the road is a finger-post (**E**) to the Hill of Alyth Walk, pointing up

a steep, rutted green track through shoulder-high gorse. At the top, when clear of the gorse, turn half-left and follow the Old Drove Road across rough grass-land, skirting the 915-foot- (279 m) high Hill of Alyth.

Aim downhill towards a line of tele-graph poles crossing diagonally across your line of sight, their tops just showing above the brow of the hill ahead. From here on, the slope of the hill offers a wide view over Alyth and Strathmore to the Sidlaws. The whole hill was long ago gifted to the people of Alyth. When you get near the line of poles, two woods are seen down the hill. Ignore the one to your right and make for the tip of the wood (**F**) directly ahead, which is approached along a track with a hedge on either side. From the corner of this wood a rough road goes down its left boundary fence, then turns first half-left along the top of a steep grazing field and then half-right to a gate onto the road coming up from Alyth. Walk down this road and take the first turning right (**G**), down through Westfield farmyard onto the Bamff road, exactly opposite the Den of Alyth car park. ☐

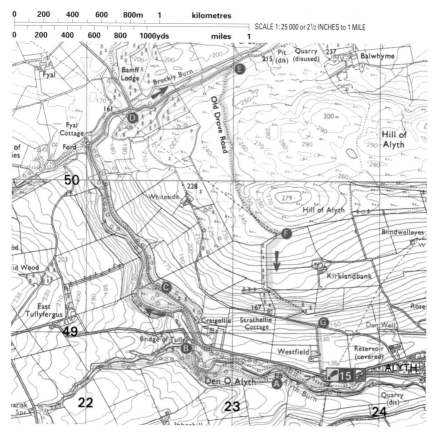

45

16 Drummond Hill and Taymouth Castle

Start:	Kenmore village
Distance:	6 miles (9.5 km)
Approximate time:	3 hours
Parking:	Kenmore car park
Refreshments:	Hotel, pub and café in Kenmore
Ordnance Survey maps:	Landranger 52 (Pitlochry & Aberfeldy), Pathfinder 322 NN 64/74 (Ben Lawers & Lower Loch Tay)

General description *This is a walk through stately parkland, where Queen Victoria walked during her honeymoon, round a golf-course beside the River Tay to visit a stone circle, and then returning through a forest to the lochside village of Kenmore. Apart from one short climb up a path in the forest, it is all level-going, and there is plenty of opportunity to wander off the described route, along parkland paths.*

Kenmore, on the shore of Loch Tay, was built as a model village by the 3rd Earl of Breadalbane in 1779 to provide his estate workers with free housing, and an excellent job he made of it. The white houses lining a sloping square with the church at the top have a more southern than Scottish aspect, while the great Gothic gateway into the grounds of Taymouth Castle reminds one of Inverary, the little town built by the Argylls to complement their castle. The walk starts through that gateway (**A**) and continues along a carriageway through the beautifully landscaped castle park, much of which is now a golf-course.

There is usually plenty of activity on the greens and fairways of the Tayside Golf Club – the players with their bulging golf bags on wheels propelled by electric motors, while others buzz about on electric buggies. In the very centre of the parkland is Taymouth Castle (**B**), built by the Earl of Breadalbane in the first half of the last century, replacing the less grand but genuine Castle of Balloch. It was completed just in time for Queen Victoria to spend her honeymoon there in 1842, when the Earl welcomed the young couple with pipers and guns and Highlanders with drawn swords. Prince Albert

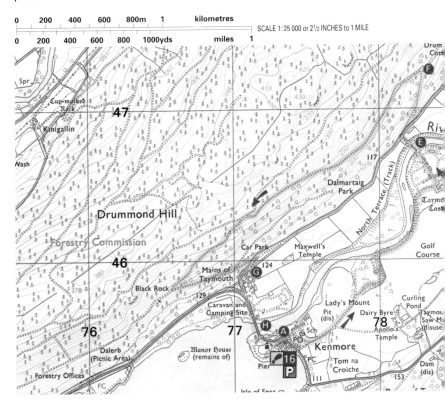

thoroughly enjoyed himself shooting lots of birds, and so taken with the place was Victoria that she seriously considered buying the estate. In the event the Prince bought Balmoral for her instead. Despite that auspicious start, the Campbells of Breadalbane were financially ruined around 1920, and today the castle is an empty shell in a beautiful setting. The golf-course was laid out in 1923 in what was originally the deer park; the deer have stayed and can be seen grazing in the rough among beech, oak, chestnut and some more exotic trees planted by the former owners. In spring the blossoming trees, the green of the fairways and the snow on the surrounding mountain tops make a scene of great beauty, as do the mellow colours of autumn. When German Ambassador to the Court of St James's, von Ribbentrop was a regular player at Tayside, and club records show that he was an accomplished golfer.

Having absorbed this historically interesting scene, walk on round the front of the castle and then up the main drive to arrive eventually at a gateway (**C**) onto the A827. Then it is but a short walk to Croftmoraig Farm and a triple stone circle (**D**), pre-dating the early Iron Age Picts.

The model village of Kenmore beside Loch Tay

The massive stones, some up to 9 feet (2.74 m) high, are in concentric circles with a maximum diameter of 50 feet (15 m). The circle is right beside the road, so one can lean on the fence to study it or go into the field through an iron gate. Return the same way to the castle, walk round behind it and then along a road past an old hangar and some derelict outbuildings to the Chinese Bridge (**E**), a cast-iron footbridge over the River Tay. On the other side, climb up a diagonal path to a grass road above the river, turn right and almost immediately left to reach a minor road running along the bottom of the forestry on Drummond Hill. Directly across the road is Rock Lodge, a ruined tower or folly, half-buried in the trees. Take a steep, little-trodden path up to the right of it. It is almost overgrown in places and a bit muddy, but after 600 yards (550 m) it comes out into a clearing beside a red waymark (**F**), pointing downhill through the forest. This was probably the first managed forest in Scotland when planted by the Breadalbanes in the early nineteenth century. Largely felled during both world wars, it was replanted in the 1940s with Scots pine, Norway spruce, Sitka spruce and Douglas fir. This last leg offers a cool, shaded walk with a U-turn at Black Rock to an exit (**G**) 1/2 mile (0.75 km) from the village. From there go downhill past a caravan site and over a bridge (**H**), where Loch Tay becomes the River Tay, and so back into Kenmore. □

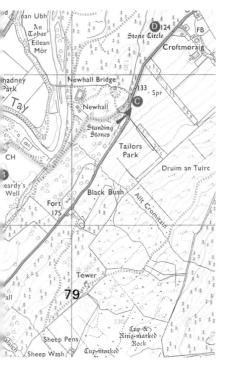

17 Glen Quaich

Start:	Amulree
Distance:	7 miles (11.25 km)
Approximate time:	3½ hours
Parking:	In Amulree
Refreshments:	Hotel and teashop, Amulree
Ordnance Survey maps:	Rangefinder 52 (Pitlochry & Aberfeldy), Pathfinder 336 NN 83/93 (Amulree)

General description Those who enjoy lake scenery will enjoy this walk which also offers a convenient opportunity to stretch one's legs if driving along the picturesque route from Crieff to Pitlochry via Sma' Glen, so much more interesting than a fast drive up the A9. The views are pleasant rather than dramatic, with the ruins of a homestead and an elegant birch-wood along the way. Although 7 miles (11.25 km) long, it is almost all on the level, with one half on a good walking track and the other half along a minor tarmac road. Gradients are insignificant. If there is time at the end of the walk, the white church in Amulree is worth a visit. It is open during daylight hours.

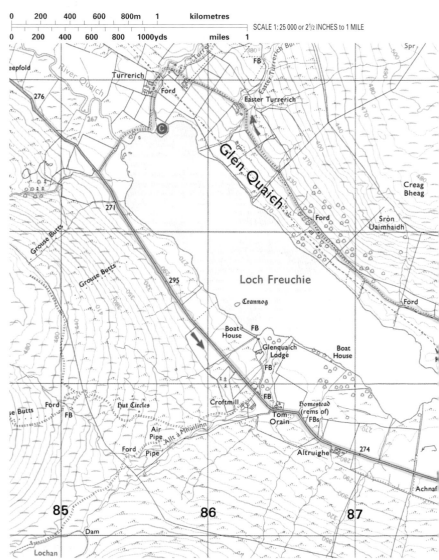

SCALE 1:25 000 or 2½ INCHES to 1 MILE

Amulree was once a junction of several drove roads, where cattle drovers rested themselves and their herds, and also the place where the clans gathered in 1715 for the Jacobite Rebellion. It sits astride one of General Wade's many military roads in the Highlands and lies at the east end of Glen Quaich, which itself is between Sma' Glen and Loch Tay. Only a few houses long, Amulree has a two-star hotel, a teashop-cum-post office and a neat white church. The glen is a long shallow bowl-shaped hanging valley, roughly bordered by the 1,000-foot (305 m) contour, with Loch Freuchie lying along most of its length, looking, on a good day, sky-blue against green hills. Although just off a scenic route, the glen is quite hidden from the road, and walking through it is likely to be a solitary exercise.

At the north end of the village, cross over the stone bridge **(A)** spanning the River Braan and turn sharp left up a private road, signposted to Kenmore with a definite 'No cars beyond this point' sign. It is, however, a pedestrian right-of-way. It passes a succession of five small copses of fir-trees and some pretty houses, all overlooked by the 1,810-foot (552 m) mass of Craig Hulich rising almost vertically from the road, so seeming more menacing than it is. Looking south, one sees the River Braan meandering and carving out ox-bows as it flows along the

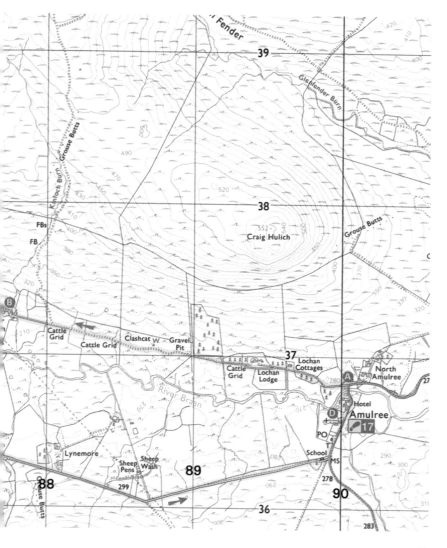

The remains of a croft in the deserted clachan of Wester Kinloch on the walk round Loch Freuchie

pastures of the valley floor. If you are staying at the Amulree Hotel you may fish the Braan and Loch Freuchie.

A mile (1.5 km) on and the foot of the loch is reached when one gets to Wester Kinloch (**B**), an old farmhouse with eaves coming down so low that they are within arm's reach. Around the house are the ruins of a small clachan, simple buildings of rough undressed stones. They are roofless, but enough of the walls remain to study the simple building techniques of the Highland crofters. From here on for a while the road becomes rutted and rocky – and would certainly damage a car.

The views over Loch Freuchie become better and more varied as the walk continues, and particularly impressive is the sight across the water of the half-punchbowl corrie of Coire a' Chearcaill, scarred by a series of gullies where winter waters have furrowed its 2,296-foot-(700 m) steep face. The loch is partially obscured for a while as the road goes up through a pleasant birch-wood to emerge for a final run down to Turrerich Farm at the loch head. A little waterside copse (**C**), fronted by a small beach, makes this end of the loch the turning point of the walk, an ideal place to stop a while and perhaps have a picnic or fish for pike. A track runs down from the farm over a stone bridge spanning the River Quaich just before it flows into the loch to meet the road going south-east back to Amulree. The road runs close to the lochside past several farms, and across the water one sees the rough road just walked in the context of the hills above it. When going north-west this road climbs to 1,750 feet (533 m) and then drops abruptly down to Loch Tay and the pretty waterside village of Kenmore, 6 miles (9.5 km) away (see Walk 16).

The white church in Amulree (**D**), *c*.1774, is a memorial to more than 300 crofters who left Glen Quaich between 1832 and 1840 for Canada, where they named their settlements Amulree and Glenquaich. Inside the church there are a number of interesting records of the emigrants as well as reports of their pioneering life in Upper Canada. A poster tells us that in 1830 agricultural workers could earn from two to three pounds a month in Canada, and land could be bought for 10 shillings (50p) an acre (0.4 ha), 20 per cent down and the balance payable over several years at low interest rates. □

18 Dunkeld, The Hermitage and Birnam

Start:	Dunkeld
Distance:	7 miles (11.25 km). Shorter versions 2¼ miles (3.75 km) and 4 miles (6.5 km)
Approximate time:	3½ hours (1 hour and 1¾ hours for shorter versions)
Parking:	The Cross, Dunkeld
Refreshments:	Hotels, restaurant, pubs and café in Dunkeld and Birnam
Ordnance Survey maps:	Landranger 52 (Pitlochry & Aberfeldy), Pathfinders 324 NO 04/14 (Dunkeld & Blairgowrie) and 323 NN 84/94 (Aberfeldy)

General description *This walk of great variety starts in the compact little cathedral town of Dunkeld, often called the Gateway to the Highlands. The route goes along the banks of the rivers Tay and Braan, takes in a famous folly and passes through two wooded glens with impressive waterfalls and rapids. It crosses an ancient bridge, climbs up over moorland and, near its end, visits a garden dedicated to Beatrix Potter, which is populated with sculptures of her animals. There is only one long uphill stretch but nothing taxing, and there are two escape points where the walk can be shortened. There may be muddy parts, so footwear should be waterproof.*

Refer to map overleaf.

The Cross stands in a small square surrounded by Dunkeld's whitewashed Little Houses, built after the destruction of the town in 1689 – following the rout of William III's army by the Jacobites at Killiecrankie – and restored in the 1950s by the National Trust for Scotland (NTS). One of them houses the Museum of the Scottish Horse Regiment. Leave the square down Cathedral Street for the cathedral, which stands on a green sward sloping down to the River Tay. It dates back to 1318 and took 200 years to build, but was ruined in just one day during the Reformation. The nave is roofless and the walls bare, but the choir has been restored and is now the parish church, where concerts can be heard on Sunday evenings during the summer. A duke of Atholl planted five European larch-seedlings in the grounds of the cathedral in 1738. They were the parents of all the widespread larch plantings carried out by the Atholls in the eighteenth and nineteenth centuries. One of the original five still grows beside the cathedral and has reached over 100 feet (30 m).

On leaving the cathedral grounds, turn sharp right outside the gates and walk down to the riverbank towards Telford's seven-arched bridge built in 1809. Cross it and on the other side take a metalled lane (**A**) which curves round the front of a white house and narrows into a path which tunnels under the A9. Follow this path onto the minor road which runs beside a caravan park. Turn right and walk into Inver to the end of its one street, which stops at the embankment of the A9. Walk up the embankment onto a narrow footpath going to the left, guarded on one side by a crash barrier. This path leads to the NTS car park (**B**) for the Hermitage Woodland Walk. From here the path is clearly marked by a series of numbered waymarks. The walk is through a glen, threaded by the River Braan in an almost perpetual turmoil of falls, rapids and swirling pools. In the eighteenth century it was laid out as a pleasure ground by the Duke of Atholl, with gravel paths surrounding little gardens of flowers among the rocks and trees. Today the gardens have gone, but it remains a pleasure woodland. There is beech from England and sycamore from France, some oak and many Dunkeld larches, a European and Japanese hybrid of the species, their seeds taken to breed high-quality timber. One Douglas fir, near the eighteenth-century Hermitage Bridge (**C**) which spans a narrow gorge, is Britain's tallest tree, topping 200 feet (61 m) and still growing.

Those wishing to take the shortest walk should cross Hermitage Bridge and take the path out of the woods to reach the A822 for a quick return back to Dunkeld.

It is here that one comes upon the folly called Ossian's Hall, which was built in 1758. Dorothy Wordsworth described it thus in 1803: 'The waterfall which we came to see warned us by a loud roaring that we must expect it; we were first however conducted into a small apartment where the gardener desired us to look at a painting of Ossian . . . the work disappeared, parting in the middle, flying asunder as by the touch of magic and lo!

we are at the entrance of a splendid room which was almost dizzy and alive with waterfalls, that tumbled in all directions – the great cascade which faced us being reflected in innumerable mirrors upon the ceiling and against the walls.' Alas the mirrors are gone, vandalised in 1821 and again in 1869 – little changes – but the roaring is still heard and, standing in a 1940s replacement folly, one looks down one of the most visually satisfying water-falls in Scotland. A great tumult of water throws itself against huge rocks and then plunges into a sharply cut venturi to be squeezed out at the other end with the thrust of a great jet engine. That scene is, of course, greatly modified after a dry spell.

Further up the walk, which keeps close to the Braan's procession of small falls and stretches of furious white-flecked, peat-stained brown water, one arrives at Ossian's Cave, another eighteenth-century folly. It is a cleverly constructed small grotto with a corbelled roof. The trees have changed to Norway spruce, with a ground cover of ferns and fungi. The red squirrel thrives in these woods, free of any competition from the grey species. From the cave the path starts to climb through commercial forestry, much wind-damaged, to cross a wider forest track. An arrow on a waymarked post points straight on, and the path, still climbing, bears away to the left until it comes out at a T-junction **(D)** with a farm road opposite a white house. Turn left past a signpost to Rumbling Bridge, thence along the edge of the forestry, over a wooden bridge and through a kissing-gate onto a field of rough grass. Follow the grass road which, like many old roads, is buttressed on either side by large stones. Running along a contour high up a hillside, this road overlooks the several square miles of dense woodland around Dunkeld and Birnam.

The Falls of Braan seen from Rumbling Bridge

Soon a gate **(E)** leads onto a road which runs downhill to Rumbling Bridge at the head of the 3-mile- (4.75 km) long Falls of the Braan. The bridge provides a viewing platform for a stretch of angry water which certainly rumbles as it pours through a narrow defile below. The road then immediately climbs uphill, passing a car park under the trees. From the back of this park, an until recently little-used footpath runs along the edge of the ravine, in which the Braan roars and foams, then turns down into the woods, crosses over a wooden footbridge recently constructed by the army, and takes you out onto the A822 **(F)**, opposite a farm road signposted 'Public Footpath to Glen Garr' and a notice saying 'Access to Balhomish and Tomgarro'.

The A822 runs straight back to Inver, providing a shortened circular walk.

To continue on the full walk, head to Balhomish Farm. This road is the longest uphill stretch of the walk, first through lush fields with scattered clumps of trees and then out onto moorland. Looking back from the top of the path one

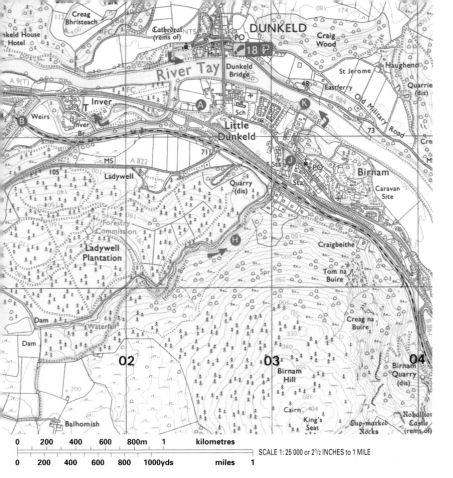

glimpses the River Tay emerging from between dark green hills. After the start of the path has forked right for Glen Garr (**G**), a farm road dips down to Balhomish, but some 200 yards (183 m) before the farm, turn left through a gate onto a cart-track across two fields and through two more gates into Ladywell Plantation. Immediately inside the woods a forest track to the right leads to a junction with the Inchewan Burn. Follow the burn downstream through Birnam Glen (**H**). It is mostly a deeply rutted track beside the water through a mix of broadleaf trees, which in places press in on the path, their branches arching overhead to form a green tunnel. At one point a sluice creates a tranquil peat-brown pool with an island of stones; a pretty place to pause perhaps to picnic. Eventually the glen path passes between two stone pillars onto a road at the apex of a hairpin bend. Take the left-hand bend and walk downhill, under a railway bridge and then under the A9 into the village of Birnam, in front of the great ornate wrought-iron gates topped with gilded lions of the Birnam Hotel. Opposite the hotel the Beatrix Potter Garden (**J**) offers a

restful diversion. It was from a house in Birnam, Heathpark, that she wrote the picture-letters to a young friend which were to become *The Tale of Peter Rabbit*. The garden paths wind past Mr and Mrs Tiggy-winkle's house, Mr Jeremy Fisher's pond and Peter Rabbit's burrow.

Leaving the garden, cross the road and walk down the lane beside the bus-shelter to Guthrie Villa that has a large B & B sign and turn left into Oak Road. On reaching a field with children's swings and slides, take the footpath on the left down to the river. Follow the sign to Birnam Oak (**K**), which is beside the path some 200 yards (183 m) on. This is a truly gigantic oak. Just above head-height, its gnarled lower limbs, outspread like the tentacles of an octopus, are supported by seven stout wooden crutches. It is said to be the last remaining tree of the ancient Birnam woods of the witches' prophesy in Shakespeare's *Macbeth*. Next to it is a sycamore, estimated to be 298 years old in 1994. From these two trees continue along the riverside path, then go up the steps by the old toll-house and over a bridge back into Dunkeld. □

19 Glen Tarken and Loch Earn

Start:	St Fillans
Distance:	7 miles (11.25 km)
Approximate time:	3½ hours
Parking:	Beside Four Seasons Hotel, St Fillans
Refreshments:	Hotels and pub in St Fillans
Ordnance Survey maps:	Landranger 51 (Loch Tay), Pathfinder 348 NN 62/72 (Loch Earn & Comrie)

General description *Starting and finishing in the lochside holiday village of St Fillans, this walk climbs up through a forest onto wide-open grouse moors which, out of the shooting season, the walker is likely to have to himself. During the shooting season, 12 August – 15 February, it is essential to keep to road-ways across grouse moors, and dogs must be kept on the lead. After winding between great crags, the path turns down into Glen Tarken, keeping company with a noisy mountain burn. A wide expanse of Loch Earn lies in front all the way down, and then there is a walk back along the lochside. This walk recommends itself to walkers who also enjoy boating or fishing, which St Fillans can provide.*

St Fillans is a holiday village of villas and cottages spread along the eastern end of Loch Earn and the head of the River Earn. It dates back to 1817 when the inhabitants of Glen Tarken were rehoused by the lochside. It is named after an Irish saint, the son of an Irish princess, who wandered the Highlands in the eighth century and died at Dundurn across the river, where there is the ruin of a chapel built in 1500 on the site of his original cell.

The walk starts at the west end of St Fillans past the Drummond Hotel, where fishing licences can be bought, and past the boat jetties as far as the Four Seasons Hotel, beside which a road climbs up to the forestry. After passing a number of villas and the tiny power-station set into the rockface, take a hairpin bend to the right (**A**), go over a railway bridge and through a small gate beside a bigger one secured with five padlocks. This road climbs for 700 feet (213 m) to a pair of boulders with prehistoric cup-marks at the end of the treeline and a ladder-stile (**B**) over a fence onto the

grouse moors. The boulders are con-spicuous, one each side of the road, but are covered with lichen, and there is only one possible cup-mark visible to the untutored eye. The fence carries a notice saying that dogs must be kept on the lead, and another saying 'Keep to roadways during the shooting season 12 August – 15 February'. The road, now more a track, continues at a much lower gradient across rough grass and bracken. It is wild, bleak terrain for the next 2¾ miles (4.5 km) as the road runs north for a while and then turns westwards between the harsh rocky faces of crags to cross the little Allt an Fhionn, 'white burn', by a small stone bridge (**C**) to meet another rough road, after ½-mile (0.75 km) coming up from Glen Tarken.

Turn left onto it and go down towards Glen Tarken Burn, passing a small tunnel and water-intake like a grating in the hillside, part of the water-catchment system. Another ½ mile (0.75 km) on, the road crosses the burn at a ford, but if it is in spate a dry-shod crossing can be made 200 yards (183 m) downstream over a wooden footbridge (**D**) instead. Over the ford turn left at a T-junction to keep parallel with the boulder-strewn Glen Tarken Burn, which can be heard tumbling through its ravine. Finally, the track comes to a gate (**E**), after which the moorland is exchanged for soft hillside pastures. A path turns off down into the ravine then over a wooden bridge and up again to Jerusalem, a ruined homestead with one small house restored, probably as a holiday home. It is worth the effort to go down to the bridge to look at a waterfall which pours over the lip of a circular stone pool. Back on the track there is now woodland to the right, and the views over Loch Earn widen out as the descent is made. Immediately below is Loch Earn Sailing Club on its little promontory and, with luck, the water will be decorated with sailing-boats, and the faint buzz of outboard motors will float up the hill.

A continuous line of richly wooded hills, with numerous summits around the 2,000-foot (610 m) mark, form the backdrop to the loch, and to the south-west Ben Vorlich at 3,231 feet (985 m) dominates the skyline. One tries not to notice the huge caravan site on the far shore, a great white block against the soft green of the hillside. Fortunately, when the trees are in leaf about a third of it is camouflaged. The road takes a zigzag course through Wester Glentarken, a cluster of ruined and renovated dwellings clinging to the steep hillside, and then crosses a dismantled railway line down to a gate **(F)** between a sheepfold and a milestone onto the A85 lochside road. The last mile (1.5 km) is along the road back to St Fillans. Lying offshore is the tiny man-made island, or crannog, of Neish. In the reign of James V (1512–42), the remnants of the Clan Neish, who were big trouble-makers in the area, took shelter on the island and were for a time safe from vengeance, but not for long. One night a party of MacNabs carried a fishing-boat overland from Loch Tay, rowed out to the island and put to the sword all but one lad who managed to escape in the dark.

In an 1860 guidebook the Drummond Arms Hotel had an advertisement which read: 'A stage coach in connection with the fast train from Edinburgh and Glasgow and the South, arrives at the hotel at twelve noon and leaves at 4 pm reaching Crieff in time to meet the evening trains North and South thus allowing visitors 4 hours for fishing or visiting the romantic scenery.' If they had stepped out they would have had just enough time to complete this walk between stage-coaches. □

20 River Earn and Laggan Hill

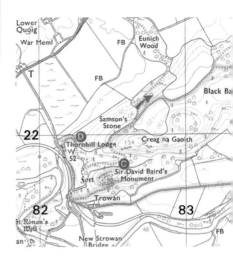

Start:	Taylor Park, Crieff
Distance:	7 miles (11.25 km)
Approximate time:	4½ hours
Parking:	Car park beside bridge in Taylor Park
Refreshments:	Hotels, restaurant, pubs and cafés in Crieff
Ordnance Survey maps:	Landranger 52 (Pitlochry & Aberfeldy), Pathfinder 349 NN 82/92 (Crieff)

General description *This walk starts from Crieff, on the south-facing foothills of the Grampians, often called the capital of Strathearn. On the outward leg the views are of the River Earn and the lush green lowlands, and on the way back the grandeur of the distant Highland hills. The gradients vary from flat to gentle slopes with one short, steep ascent. Most of the way is through woodland with many scenic gaps between. It can be muddy in a few places after rain, but there is no rough terrain.*

On weekdays during the pheasant-shooting season, from the end of October to February, telephone Mr Archie McDiarmid on 0764 652369 to inquire if there is shooting on his land between the tent-site by Thornhill Lodge and Laggan Hill. As there are also roe-deer on his land, dogs are not allowed at any time even on the lead.

In the eighteenth-century, Crieff was a cattle-trading centre at the end of drove roads from the Highlands. With the coming of the railway in Victorian times it became a fashionable spa town with its Strathearn Hydropathic, now the Crieff Hydro. Today it is a popular holiday centre, being near Perth, the Trossacks, Lough Earn and Loch Tay. There are a number of good walks in the area; this one combines two of them with some new ground in-between.

To get to the start point follow West High Street, then turn right onto Comrie Street. Just before the war memorial, go west down Milnab Street to Taylor Park. Cross the bridge over Turret Burn and immediately turn left at the signpost 'Lady Mary's Walk' **(A)** and continue along the path through woods and under a derelict railway bridge beside the Turret. After passing through a gate, the path leaves the water's edge for a short while before taking up its position alongside the River Earn. Here the path broadens out to run for a mile (1.5 km) through an avenue of beeches, with the broad, tumbling river keeping it company.

After passing several little riverside beaches, the path turns right through a gap **(B)** in the old railway embankment and goes through a kissing-gate onto a rather rocky bit of path to a T-junction with a muddy farm road. To the right the road goes back to Crieff, so turn left to a small clearing in the trees and thence through a gate to a path running along the edges of a number of fields. From here in the distance straight ahead can be seen a high hillock topped by a stone needle – Sir David Baird's Monument **(C)**, the halfway mark on this walk. The fields lie at the foot of a range of small, totally tree-covered hills. The walk makes its return journey along their summits.

The path keeps on virtually straight to Trowan, a small stone farmhouse with roses up the wall. A short driveway from the house comes out onto a country lane which runs downhill to the A85, midway between Crieff and Comrie. Walk down this road a few yards to a little lodge, beside which is the start of the steep path up to the monument. A copy of Cleopatra's Needle on the Thames embankment, it was erected in 1832 in memory of Sir David Baird, a hero of the Indian wars.

This commanding hill, crowned with dedicated woodland of oak and birch, was formerly the site of Tom-a-Chastile, a medieval castle and stronghold of the

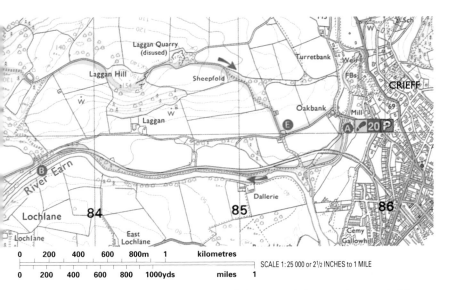

0   200   400   600   800m   1   kilometres

0   200   400   600   800   1000yds   miles   1

SCALE 1: 25 000 or 2½ INCHES to 1 MILE

Earls of Strathearn. When workmen were erecting the monument they found a subterranean chamber containing human bones and gold and silver ornaments. The return leg of the walk is along an old scenic carriage-drive lined with lime-trees which climbs up through the woods near the monument and runs along the north edge of Creag na Gaoith and Black Bank and then down to Loch Monzievaird and Ochtertyre, until recently the seat of the Murray family. Unhappily, the last of the family to occupy the house gambled the estate away and ended up living in one room before taking his life. The house has changed hands twice since then. To get onto this carriageway, now an overgrown track, return to the little lodge and walk down the road to Thornhill Lodge, which has a 'Tenting Field' sign beside it. The road through this small campsite is the start of the old carriageway to Ochtertyre, and the owners are quite happy for people to walk through it, but it would be courteous to ask if they are there.

At the far end of the site the old carriageway enters the woods below the monument and becomes impassable, so step over a low wire fence (D) into a field and walk uphill, keeping near the stone wall round the edge of the woods until, at the summit, you come to Samson's Stone, a glacial boulder that never rolled down into the valley below. By the stone one can get back onto the now grass-covered carriageway which runs along the edge of the hill. From this point there is a wide-angle panorama westward to Comrie with its white-spired church and Ben Vorlich beyond, while to the north is the whole sweep of the Grampians with

Ochtertyre sitting on the wooded lower slopes of the foothills. This three-storey Georgian house to a design by the Adam brothers has an imposing pavilion front and is an unusual sight in Scotland. At the first fork in the road, keep to the right on a muddy path overgrown by ferns. In a while it turns right and then left, leaving the woods briefly so there are again views north. At the next fork again keep right. The left-hand path is the remains of the carriageway where it descended the hill on its way to the house. The right fork goes up through mixed forestry to a large pond totally overgrown with trees, some fallen over into the water so that it looks like a miniature mangrove swamp. At one time it was a open expanse of water on which local children sailed home-made rafts.

Keep the pond on your left and take a path straight ahead which goes uphill alongside a stone wall. This leads to Laggan Hill in the middle of a mixed wood with a seat on the way. The path remains distinct – although not shown on the map at this point – as it curves round the summit and then starts on a long slope down, past an overgrown, disused quarry, with many twists and turns to the outskirts of Crieff. Where the path remains high up there are good oblique views over the whole of the town. Finally the path emerges from the woods onto a proper road for a short distance to crossroads. A sign points ahead to Lady Mary's Walk. Here turn left beside Turret Lodge (E) and walk through a new housing estate to the road junction by the Oakbank public house. From there it is only a few yards back over the bridge to the car park.   □

21 Ben Chonzie

Start:	Coishavachan, Glen Lednock
Distance:	6 miles (9.5 km)
Approximate time:	4 hours
Parking:	By schoolhouse, Coishavachan
Refreshments:	None
Ordnance Survey maps:	Landranger 51 (Loch Tay), Pathfinders 348 NN 62/72 (Loch Earn & Comrie) and 335 NN 63/73 (Upper Loch Tay)

General description *Ben Chonzie is a Munro that almost anybody in good health can climb because although its rough road deteriorates into a track, it does go nearly to the top, and the gradient is, by hillwalking standards, quite gentle. The last 400 feet (122 m) or so are on mossy grass, and the summit is almost flat, so there is no last minute scramble. It is worth climbing because it is the highest summit in the area of Crieff and Comrie, and is a good follow-on to an easy walk through the picturesque Glen Lednock, to which its empty moorland slopes are a great contrast. However, because of its featureless shape, the summit should be avoided when in mist or cloud by those who are not adept at using a compass.*

During the grouse-shooting season, 12 August – 15 February, ring 0764 670959 to check on access.

Glen Lednock, from the track up Ben Chonzie

The popular route to the summit of Ben Chonzie starts at the hamlet of Coishavachan beside the road through Glen Lednock just before it reaches Loch Lednock Reservoir. Park on a triangular layby opposite the old schoolhouse and walk up a short road to a group of white cottages. A gate **(A)** at their right-hand end leads onto a rough road signposted as a right-of-way to Ardtalnaig, way over the hill on the shore of Loch Tay. Keep on it as far as it goes. To start with, it rises gently past a sheepfold on the right and then crosses a wooden bridge over the heavily boulder-strewn bed of Invergeldie Burn. There are always likely to be more boulders than water in this burn because the water authority extracts water from it further up.

As you walk higher and higher the view back down Glen Lednock gets better, while close at hand the tree-filled ravine through which the burn flows provides a

final slash of green against the unremitting heather of the grouse moors ahead. A mile (1.5 km) from the start, the track makes a couple of hairpin bends, dipping down to the burn and then steeply up again by the intake marked on the map. This is really more like a small dam with a large grating along its rim into which the water coming down the burn disappears underground to feed the reservoir. Normally only a trickle of water leaks out from this concrete barrier to be lost among the great weather-bleached boulders below the dam.

The walk goes on relentlessly uphill along the track, which can be seen curving up the south-western slope of the ben for about 2 miles (3.25 km) ahead. A few rock outcrops and a line of grouse butts break the pattern of the blanket heather. Looking to the south, the nearby crags of Creag na h-Iolaire present an interesting line of sharp peaks and dome tops, while ahead and a little to the right the isolated outcrop of Creag Gharbh looks as if it might be your summit, but is not. The broad smooth bulk of Ben Chonzie rises to your left, and its 3,053-foot (931 m) summit is well out of sight beyond the brow which you see. Along the way the road dips down to a ford **(B)**, which is the point where the right-of-way to Ardtalnaig via Glen Almond turns off north through the Invergeldie Pass. From here on, the road deteriorates into a rough and rocky track.

At the 2,624-foot (800 m) contour the track ends **(C)** with a little cairn as a full stop. From here turn half-left, take a compass bearing on the wire-and-post fence and continue uphill towards it. If in doubt about the weather on the way up, it is a good idea to leave some marker on the fence where you meet it to provide a back-bearing from there to the track. Aim directly for a small rock outcrop by the fence, if you can see it. This fence runs all the way to the summit which, because of the slow slope and flat top, is not seen until it is almost reached, where it is marked by a cairn. Parallel with the fence but some way from it, a line of small cairns also marches to the summit, so you can wander over the grass and moss between the two without danger of getting lost. Make sure you do not lose sight of these markers in poor weather as the route to the summit makes a 90° turn on the way.

From the summit you look down into Glen Almond, Glen Quaich (but not Loch Freuchie) and Loch Tay, then round to the west Ben Vorlich is prominent, and to the south you might even see as far as Stirling.

Return the way you came. But there remains the problem of finding out when to leave the line of fence or cairns on the way down to hit the end of the track up from Glen Lednock. At the marker left on the way up, take a reciprocal bearing – by adding 180° to the original bearing on the ascent – and then walk on that bearing until you meet the track.

On the way back Glen Lednock below offers the walker a much more pleasant view than the bare hillslope did on the way up.   ☐

22 West Dron and Glenearn Hills

Start:	West Dron
Distance:	6 miles (9.5 km)
Approximate time:	3½ hours
Parking:	Off road near West Dron Farm
Refreshments:	None
Ordnance Survey maps:	Landranger 58 (Perth and Kinross), Pathfinder 361 NO 01/11 (Bridge of Earn & Dunning)

General description This is a fine panoramic walk along the rim of a plateau commanding views over half of Perthshire, and it includes a visit to the well-defined shape of a prehistoric hill fort. At the beginning of the last century, when the young Walter Scott was riding his pony for the first time on his own, he arrived at a high point on this walk and wrote afterwards: 'I recollect pulling up the reins not meaning to do so, and gazing on the scene before me, as if I had been afraid it would shift like those in a theatre before I could distinctly observe its parts or convince myself it was real.' He was on Dron Hill which inspired a famous passage of description in the first chapter of The Fair Maid of Perth. What better reason to walk it?

West Dron Farm is ¾ mile (1.25 km) west of the M90 and 2½ miles (4 km) from the Bridge of Earn by road. It is a question of personal judgement where to pull off the road and park before reaching the farm, where there is space but an unambiguous 'No cars No parking' sign. You may, however, walk down the lane in front of the farm which is a right-of-way to a couple of cottages at the foot of Wallace Road, also a right-of-way, which goes over Dron Hill to Glenfarg. It was on this road that Walter Scott was riding his pony.

Turn up Wallace Road **(A)**, which is now a typical farm road, until coming to a track off to the right **(B)** which climbs up to the ruined buildings of Mundie. Follow this track to within about 200 yards (183 m) of Mundie and then climb round the north face of West Dron Hill. From its grassy hilltop at 961 feet (293 m), you look across the Earn and Tay to the scarps of Moncreiffe Hill and Kinnoull Hill, the latter with its tower folly perched on the edge of a rock ledge, high above the road to Dundee. A bit of Perth is visible to the left

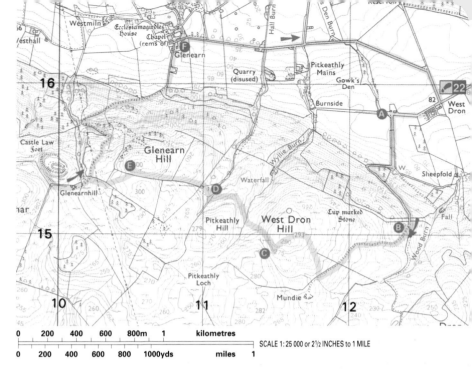

of Kinnoull Hill and – what Scott did not see – almost immediately below is the broad ribbon of the M90 motorway snaking towards the city. Altogether, the panorama stretches from Dundee in the east to the start of the Grampians in the west. Some trees have been planted recently on West Dron Hill, so in time it will look quite different.

Come off the hill, heading south. The way down is over rough grass and some scree, at the bottom of which is the surprise sight of a caravan (C) which, on closer inspection, turns out to be a total wreck. But it serves as a marker-point at which to turn west to round Pitkeathly Hill. A grass track can be picked up, but the fence by the tiny Hall Burn ahead is an obstacle which just has to be climbed over. The best place is by a patch of trees (D) where the ground on one side of the fence is higher than the other, providing a natural stile. Then keep going west up a sheep-track along the north side of an old drystone wall running west in the dip between the summit of Glenearn Hill and the 984-foot (300 m) point south of it. From here the shape of Castle Law fort can now be seen. Head for an opening in the wall (E) at the bottom of the Glenearn slope and take the sheep-track diagonally across to the left-hand pylon of the two seen directly ahead. Keep on towards the end of a stand of trees, where a track runs left to Glenearnhill, a ruined farm steading. A fairly obvious track goes on from there to circle round below the fort to an

iron gate which is extremely stiff to open. When through it, keep to the right for a few yards to avoid boggy ground, before striking up to the top of the fort.

This hill fort had two concentric walls with timber-laced ramparts, and there is evidence of vitrification where the intense heat generated by wood-burning fused stones together into almost solid rock. The site is thought to have first been used at the time of Agricola's campaign and later to have been partially rebuilt. A bank-and-ditch fortification was erected in the Dark Ages or Pictish times, and then in medieval times it may have been used as an enclosure for cattle. Although the site is now only grassy mounds and depressions, it is obvious that it was once an extensive and probably important fort. The reason is clear; it gives magnificent views to the west past Crieff and Comrie and of the mouths of all the great glens opening up to the north, with most of Strathearn and Strath Tay discernible. Eastwards the view takes in Angus and Dundee. All this is dependant, of course, on clear air. Retrace your steps to the iron gate and walk round to the start of the road at Glenearnhill which makes the steep twisting descent to the valley floor. You will pass an enclosure of rhododendrons, a strange sight in the middle of nowhere. Reaching level ground, the road passes a small quarry just before Glenearn. From here it bends to the right (F), before continuing a good mile back to West Dron. □

23 Ben Lawers

Start:	NTS Visitor Centre
Distance:	6 miles (9.5 km). Shorter version 1½ miles (2.5 km)
Approximate time:	5 hours (1½ hours for shorter version)
Parking:	NTS car park
Refreshments:	None
Ordnance Survey maps:	Rangefinder 51 (Loch Tay), Pathfinders 335 NN 63/73 (Upper Loch Tay) and 322 NN 64/74 (Ben Lawers and Lower Loch Tay)

General description Ben Lawers is the highest mountain in Perthshire at 3,984 feet (1,214 m) and is famous for its alpine flora, much of which is found nowhere else in Britain. To save the flora from the acquisitiveness of botanists and alpine gardeners, the National Trust for Scotland (NTS) have bought 8,000 acres (3,240 ha) on the mountain's southern flank. An equal menace were the sheep belonging to farmers with grazing rights on the slopes. They are still there today, so the NTS have fenced in a broad area of 62 acres (25 ha) on either side of the Burn of Edramucky and the track leading to the summit to keep out both sheep and deer. There are therefore two walks, one to the summit and the other along the nature trail within the fences. The NTS have a capacious car park at the start of the path and an interpretive centre.

Keep in mind that the longer version of the walk contains some scrambling over boulders and a fairly strenuous descent. Especially, you should be aware of the imminent weather conditions. If in doubt, seek advise from the ranger or one of the staff at the visitor centre.

For both the nature trail and the summit track, start along a duckboard walkway over boggy ground to a stile **(A)** in the perimeter fence of the nature trail area. Here the path divides, left for the summit, right for the trail which has six sections with numbered posts. Take the right-hand path.

The nature trail is no more than a gentle stroll up an ascent of about 656 feet (200 m) and allows study of the plant and bird life in some detail. The most common birds in this area are meadow pipit, skylark and wheatear, while red grouse may be seen and heard protecting their territories among the heather. From early June to the end of August green-veined white, small pearl-bordered fritillary, small heath, small mountain ringlet and small tortoiseshell butterflies may be seen in that order through the three months. A little gorge gives shelter to woodland plants such as wood anemones and primroses. The bed of the burn running through the gorge consists of garnet mica-schist, the red crystals of which will be seen protruding from boulders along the path. Erosion of this soft rock has left harder bands to form a number of small waterfalls. From the top of the trail, where it meets the route **(B)** to the summit, a dam is visible which diverts most of the water in the burn through a tunnel into Lochan na Lairige. From there it is taken, together with water from other burns, down into Loch Tay via the Finlarig power-station near Killin.

Walkers wishing to return down to the car park should take the left-hand track – looking up from the visitor centre – which is used by those walking directly to the summit but marked 'Nature Trail' on the map.

To continue on the longer walk to the summit, another 2,000 feet (610 m) higher and 3½ miles (5.5 km) further, is a much tougher proposition. It is a long plod with some steep sections, and in places the path is rough enough to necessitate watching one's feet rather than the view, but fit young people think nothing of going up and down in four to five hours. When the weather closes in, Ben Lawers, and for that matter any other high mountain, should be left alone. Not only is there the possibility of straying from the path and becoming disorientated but also the risk of hypothermia if caught out in wet, windy conditions when tired and inadequately clad. Whatever the weather beside Loch Tay at the foot of the mountain, the temperature at the summit will be at least 7° C colder, further aggravated by wind-chill, for there is rarely a lack of wind at the top of a mountain. The path to the summit is clear by the fact that it is so well worn. From time to time the NTS reroute sections where erosion has become too great. These diversions are always clearly marked.

After leaving the nature trail area over another stile, the path heads due north to below the ruins of shielings **(C)**, turns east and then starts to steepen across a rather uncomfortable section of soft, brittle, broken schist to run along the edge of Coire a' Chonnaidh where the going is

The final assault to the summit of Ben Lawers, Perthshire's highest mountain, from the saddle

better, being a hard, gravelly-type surface. Now enough height has been gained for sweeping views of Loch Tay as far as Killin to the west. There follows a steep climb over two hillocks of Beinn Ghlas **(D)**, the penultimate summit which up to now has hidden the top of Ben Lawers from view. On this stretch the ground is covered with loose stones and boulders which have to be climbed around, and at times it may be necessary to use hands as well as feet. Beyond Beinn Ghlas there is a drop down to a narrow, windy, grass-covered saddle between two corries.

The final assault is up through another area of broken schist past boulders and one last steep climb onto a small level plateau with a rocky bump which is the summit **(E)**. The ascent may be tedious for those not so fit, but on a fine day with clear air the reward is great. The eye takes in a view which for grandeur, variety and extent is possibly without equal in Britain. Mountain summits line the horizon in all directions from Ben Nevis to the Cairngorms, from Ben Lomond to Beinn-y-Ghlo, even to the Paps of Jura. In the immediate vicinity is the Ben Lawers massif itself, covering 42 square miles (110 sq km) with eight tops above 3,000 feet (915 m). There is a triangulation pillar and an indicator panel; this was recently removed but will almost certainly have been replaced. The descent by the same route is strenuous on the knees so should be taken steadily, both to enjoy the alternative view and also for safety. It is easier to lose one's balance hurrying down than walking up, and to slip on a wet grass slope could be dangerous near the edge of a corrie. In the late summer there is the chance to refresh oneself near the end of the walk with wild blaeberries (bilberries) which grow just above the nature trail. ☐

24 Glen Tilt

Start:	Gateway to Blair Castle
Distance:	12½ miles (20 km)
Approximate time:	5½ hours
Parking:	In Blair Atholl
Refreshments:	Hotels, pubs and café in Blair Atholl
Ordnance Survey maps:	Landranger 43 (Braemar), Pathfinders 294 NN 86/96 (Blair Atholl & Killiecrankie) and 281 NN 87/97 (Glen Tilt)

General description *This is a long walk through a Highland glen alongside a turbulent river overlooked by impressive mountains. The route here recommended requires no special clothing, but be prepared for some stretches of wet grass and a little mud. The way out is all uphill, but gently so, at a gradient of less than 400 feet (122 m) in 5 miles (8 km). Glen Tilt runs roughly due north and provides a right-of-way from Blair Castle at Blair Atholl for some 16 miles (26 km) to the Linn of Dee and thence by road a few miles further to Braemar. For the leisurely walker the route offers a day among trees, hills and waterfalls, away from the sound of all traffic. The circuit described here differs from the one in the Glen Tilt Trail leaflet in two respects. It keeps closer to the river, which is itself an attraction, and it avoids what would otherwise be a lot of forestry walking. It also avoids using paths which are sometimes closed to the public when a rifle range is in use.*

Refer to map overleaf.

Blair Castle is one of the most visited stately homes in Scotland – a fairy-tale, white, towered edifice. It has some thirteenth-century parts but has been continuously altered down the centuries, and its present exterior is almost totally Victorian romantic. The village too was mostly built in the latter part of the last century, with matching granite buildings in the same Victorian style. It remains the seat of the Dukes of Atholl whose ancestors were responsible for clothing Perthshire, much of which they owned, in its mantle of trees.

Start by walking up the main drive to Blair Castle and about halfway turn off to the right **(A)** along a wooded footpath which runs across the north end of the caravan park. This leads to East Lodge on the road from Old Bridge of Tilt to Old Blair. Go through the gateway beside the lodge onto the estate road **(B)** up the glen. Although rather a rough road for cars, which must pay £5 to use it, it is a good walking road and enables those in a hurry to step out. On the left for the first mile (1.5 km) are the sloping fields of the castle's Home Farm, where cattle are grazed in winter, but driven higher up the glen in summer. To the right, the river runs in a deep ravine blanketed by trees, but it becomes extremely noisy by a bend in the road, above where the triple Falls of Fender pour into the Tilt.

By now the trees have closed in on the road, and soon there is a yellow arrow waymark pointing up a footpath to the left **(C)**. That is the way given in local literature, but it leads through forestry, past the rifle range and then again through forestry well away from the Tilt. Stay on the estate road, which keeps near the water and then crosses onto the east bank by Cumhann-leum Bridge **(D)**. From here on it runs along the riverbank through the birch and oak of Dalginross Wood, reaching open hillside just beyond Gilbert's Bridge. So far only one small farmhouse-turned-holiday home, Croft-more, has been passed, but now beside the road there is first a large complex of sheep-dips and then Auchgobhal, a shepherd's house surrounded by sheep-pens. When dipping or shearing are in progress there can be several hundred sheep gathered here, and their bleating is heard loud and clear from a long way off. All along this section of the walk the Tilt is showing off its prowess as a rock sculptor. When not in spate the great stone slabs lining its sides are well exposed to show the artistic whirls incised in them, and in midstream serried ranks of rock pinnacles look like model alpine ranges.

Next along the road is Marble Lodge; no marble here, just a small cottage which got its name from an outcrop of green marble further upstream. It has been extracted on a small scale since 1815, and in 1817 fetched one guinea (£1.05) per cubic foot (0.03 cu m). The great fireplace in Blair Castle's entrance hall is made of marble from this site. The road crosses back onto the other bank over Gaw's Bridge **(E)**, the turning point of the walk. It is so named after a man who kept a pub nearby, when there were several hundred souls living in the glen, and no doubt it also served the cattle drovers who used this route in the days before the clearances put sheep on all the hills. By walking 200 yards (183 m) beyond the

The River Tilt, which keeps the walker company most of the time through Glen Tilt

bridge one gets a good impression of the U-shaped glacial valley of upper Glen Tilt.

Returning along the same road, one passes a spring **(F)** on the steep roadside bank, which is known as the Queen's Well after Victoria, who so enjoyed its water when she stayed at Blair Castle. Shortly after, a post with a yellow arrow marks an area of lint pools **(G)**. Today they are barely discernible, sometimes water-logged depressions beside the road – remnants of the flax-growing days in the glen. The flax was soaked in the pools, which were made by damming a hillside burn or spring. After a three-week soak it was beaten to separate the fibres from the core, then the womenfolk span the fibres in their cottages, several families supplying one weaver's loom. Highland linen was of a high quality, but cheap imports of Indian cotton made linen production uneconomical at about the same time as the sheep-farming landowners drove the cattle and most of the population from the glens around the middle of the last century.

The marker at the lint pools points to the old grass track right-of-way which runs uphill above Auchgobhal. Follow it into the birch-wood of Dalginross. This slender tree is found all over the Highlands and was popular for making domestic and agricultural implements, while its bark was used for tanning and its small branches and twigs for thatching. For some it still provides an alternative to whisky. A tap is knocked about an inch into the trunk in the spring, from which a gallon of rising sap is gathered and then fermented into a potent wine.

The grass path rises out of Dalginross Wood onto open ground, passing just above Croftmore and then through the eastern edge of Leathad Mór Wood. At a junction with a path going deeper into the wood, fork left, cross a small ford and emerge from the trees onto open fields in front of Kincraigie Farm **(H)**, from where there is a clear view up and down the glen and away to the west. Looking back one sees the high hills between which the Tilt has flowed with Beinn Dearg's shapely dome predominant.

From here on it is a downhill walk by a minor road with superb oblique views of Blair Castle surrounded by trees and lying like a pearl on a green velvet cloth. At a junction with the road from Tirinie, turn right quite steeply downhill to the hamlet of Fenderbridge. A delightful old stone bridge takes you over the Fender Burn, and on the other side of it, at another T-junction, turn right again down to Old Bridge of Tilt. A right turn uphill in the village goes over the Tilt to the gateway by East Lodge. The circuit is complete but for the walk back into Blair Atholl via the castle driveway. □

25 Choinneachain Hill, Glen Turret

Start:	Loch Turret Reservoir
Distance:	7 miles (11.25 km)
Approximate time:	4 hours
Parking:	Reservoir car park
Refreshments:	None
Ordnance Survey maps:	Landranger 52 (Pitlochry & Aberfeldy), Pathfinders 349 NN 82/92 (Crieff) and 348 NN 62/72 (Loch Earn & Comrie) and 335 NN 63/73 (Upper Loch Tay) and 336 NN 83/93 (Amulree)

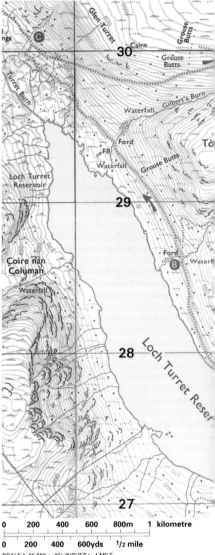

0 200 400 600 800m 1 kilometre

0 200 400 600yds ¹/2 mile

SCALE 1: 25 000 or 2¹/2 INCHES to 1 MILE

General description *This is a fairly long walk along hard tracks out on open moorland well away from habitation and probably people too as it is not a well-known route. The outward leg runs beside a loch and then swings round to climb quite steeply to a hill with a view, after which the rest is downhill over bleak grouse moors. Taken steadily, it is suitable for a family wanting some good exercise. However, no dogs may be taken on this walk, and walkers must keep to the route.*

A private road, open to cars during daylight hours, runs alongside the Turret Burn north-west of Crieff to the car park by the dam on Loch Turret Reservoir. It passes the Falls of Turret, which are worth stopping to look at. From the car park, walk to the dam and cross over the stile at the right-hand end onto the track which runs beside the loch. There is a notice which categorically states 'No dogs' and another saying 'Sheep farm. Walkers must adhere strictly to the hill roads and not detour from them for any reason. By order'. Because of these instructions, one cannot take a few obvious and practical short-cuts, with the result that the walk covers four Pathfinder maps, just cutting across the corners of three of them.

The ground on this side of the loch is covered with heather, and rocky outcrops tower above the track. On the other side of the loch is mostly grass and bracken. The first burn coming down from Choinneachain Hill, the destination of the walk, is crossed by a wooden sleeper **(A)**. The track undulates but as yet is not steep.

Ahead, beyond the head of the loch, is the slightly rounded summit of Ben Chonzie, the destination of Walk 21. A little further along you come to a lovely little waterfall **(B)** at the bottom of Allt Bhaltair, dropping down between Choinneachain and Tòn Eich. It is set among a few lonely trees, silver birch and rowans. Just beyond the falls, a track takes off up the valley but should be ignored as it soon peters out. Another 200 yards (183 m) on and some fences and rhododendron bushes are evidence of former habitation. It was here that Glen Turret House was submerged when the dam was built in the 1960s, and its remains can be seen in dry periods

when the water-level is low. Gilbert's Burn is crossed by stepping stones, and here again there are a few trees. Once past the head of the loch, the track runs briefly in line with Turret Burn, and the ground is covered in little hillocks, probably glacial moraine deposit.

Just before some old shielings, the track comes to a T-junction **(C)** where you turn right; the left track soon fades out. To start with, this route doubles back on the outward one and then swings away to climb steeply northwards to Auchnafree Hill; a short spur going off left must be ignored as it just serves some grouse

Loch Turret Reservoir and Choinneachain Hill

26 Schiehallion

Start:	Braes of Foss
Distance:	6 miles (9.5 km)
Approximate time:	5 hours
Parking:	Forestry car park, Braes of Foss
Refreshments:	None
Ordnance Survey maps:	Landranger 42 (Loch Rannoch), Pathfinder 308 NN 65/75 (Kinloch Rannoch & Schiehallion)

General description Schiehallion is pleasant to look upon and with its euphonious name and conical summit

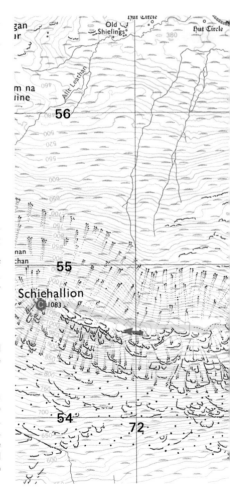

butts. On reaching the ford **(D)** over Gilbert's Burn, the path changes its mind and makes a sharp turn south towards Tòn Eich. A bit of a zigzag follows and then the way bends round the 2,384-foot (727 m) summit of Tòn Eich, dips down and heads up the side of Choinneachain Hill. This is high grouse country of heather and peat-bog with a little grass in-between. The climb up the side of Choinneachain is moderately steep, and on the 2,460-foot (750 m) contour another track crosses from left to right. Go left **(E)** to a cairn, which is about 10 feet (3 m) tall, on the edge of the summit plateau. At this, the highest point on the walk, the fertile valley of Strathearn opens out ahead, and beyond are the low Ochil Hills. On a completely clear day you will see Perth, while Crieff lies at your feet at the bottom of its wooded knock.

Now walk on eastwards for about 400 yards (366 m) to a much older cairn, Càrn Chainichin or King Kenneth's Cairn, which stands on the edge of the steep escarpment of Corrie Barvick. It was built about 1003 in memory of the son of King Duff, who was killed in the Battle of Monzievaird that year. Kenneth was buried on Iona, as were many other Scottish kings. Descending from Kenneth's Cairn, the track curves along the edge of the rocky face of Creag Chaisean, with Stonefield Hill rising further away. The track now runs downhill towards Barvick Burn, and the best of the scenery is left behind as height is lost. Where the path bends closest to Loch Turret one might be tempted to take a short-cut towards Allt Choinneachain to regain the lochside track near the dam. But, being mindful of the 'By order' sign, one must make a great detour along the track round an area of rock outcrops and grouse butts, before turning west to approach the dam from Glen Turret. □

might loosely be described as the Mount Fuji of Perthshire. It is the focus of attention from several well-visited view-points, chief among them Queen's View on Loch Tummel. But the long walk up its whaleback slope to the summit is far from pleasant. Half of the 3-mile (4.75 km) ascent is up a rough path over moorland, the other half extremely hard-going over ankle-wrenching, angular quartzite rocks. Nevertheless, it is a popular and some-times crowded walk, but strong walking-boots are essential, and clothing should be suitable for a cold summit at 3,553 feet (1,083 m). Carrying a compass is a further sensible precaution. Getting to the top needs stamina and is more of a challenge than fun. Dogs that are not used to walking on rough ground will not enjoy the top of Schiehallion any more than non-hillwalkers will.

A good safety idea and a way to avoid being disheartened by the false summits that Schiehallion presents the walker is to study them before going up. This can be done by driving to the highest point along the B849 south of Tummel Bridge to look at Schiehallion from above Loch Kinardochy. From there the track is visible winding up to the ridge, and you can look along its whole length to the summit, counting the false ones in-between.

In 1774 the astronomer Reverend Nevile Maskelyne started experiments on Schiehallion to determine the density of the earth by observing the deflection that the mountain caused to a plumb-line. He concluded, mistakenly, that the earth's density was 4.5 times that of water. What became of more importance, and of greater interest to walkers, was that his assistant, Charles Hutton, surveyed the

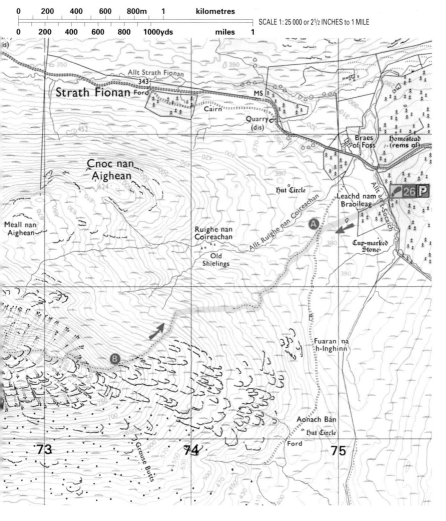

The long incline from Braes of Foss to the summit of Schiehallion which is often shrouded in mist

mountain and drew lines connecting all points of one height, so giving us the contour line. The plaque by the forestry car park tells this story more fully.

The popular path to the top starts from the Braes of Foss forestry car park, which is entered by the memorial plaque to the Astronomer Royal Nevile Maskelyne, beside the Schiehallion Road from Kinloch Rannoch. Cross over a stile by a footprint sign and then a wooden footbridge and follow the path alongside the forestry fence to open moorland. From here the path forms a distinct earth-coloured scar running at a gentle incline through the heather and then zigzagging steeply up the flank to meet the east ridge about one third of the way up it. Not only is the path clear to see, but in the summer there will be lots of colourful figures walking up and down ahead of you, so there is no chance of going wrong. It is quite heavy going gaining 1,377 feet (420 m) in about 1¼ miles (2 km). Early on, the path passes a cairn **(A)** and, when it meets a track running from left to right, keep straight ahead and, where it forks, keep to the left.

After a long slog, the ridge **(B)** is reached at 2,460 feet (750 m), where the heather gives way to rock. From here on, sharp, angular quartzite lumps of rock all the way up to the summit make punishing walking. Even dogs can get distressed picking their way between sharp rock with almost no level surface to walk on. There is no path, but the right direction is marked by a line of cairns, and it is essential to make your way from one to another in mist or low cloud as the ridge narrows towards the summit, and the sides are almost sheer. Not only is it uncomfortable but, if you do not know where the summit is, it will be dis-heartening, as there are several mocking, false summits on the way.

If the whole mountain is likened to a whale, then the summit **(C)** is where its spout would be. After the effort of getting there, the scenery is remarkable, taking in the Shepherds of Etive by Loch Rannoch and Ben Nevis beyond that. In the east you see the Tummel valley, the mountains of Atholl above Blair Atholl and, on a good day, the Cairngorms. Nearer-to are the five Munros of the Ben Lawers massif. However, if the weather is not good, there is no point in walking all the way to the summit unless you are a 'Munro bagger'. There are amply rewarding views from where the heather meets the ridge without going out onto the rock. Return to the car park by the same route. □

27 Creagh Dhubh, Glen Lyon

Start:	Invervar
Distance:	4½ miles (7.25 km)
Approximate time:	4 hours
Parking:	Invervar
Refreshments:	None
Ordnance Survey maps:	Landranger 51 (Loch Tay), Pathfinder 322 NN 64/74 (Ben Lawers and Lower Loch Tay)

General description Glen Lyon is the longest glen in Scotland and arguably the most beautiful. Threaded by the turbulent River Lyon and hemmed in by incredibly steep hills, several of them Munros, its wild beauty is best appreciated from some high point. This walk takes the energetic to just such a point. It involves a steep walk which zigzags 1,164 feet (355 m) above the river. There are no difficulties but, because of the steepness of the climb, one needs to have had some practice at hillwalking to enjoy it. Parts can be boggy, so good footwear is needed.

If you wish to visit the lint mill in Invervar at point **E** during the deer-stalking season, from 1 September or earlier to 15 February, telephone the North Chesthill estate on 0887 877235 first to check whether the branch path to the mill is closed for shooting.

The walk starts 5 miles (8 km) west of Fortingall at Invervar, a hamlet so small it is easy to drive past it. Park by the telephone-box on the left of the road and walk back a few yards to a small lane **(A)** running down through a wood to the riverbank. Cross over the big wooden bridge, from which, at times, leaping salmon may be seen. On the other side a tree-covered hill rises abruptly, seeming to block the way. Follow the lane in a hook round to the left, then right and past an aluminium gate **(B)** to walk through the trees parallel with the river. Carry on through another aluminium gate in a

0	200	400	600	800m	1	kilometres	
0	200	400	600	800	1000yds	miles	1

SCALE 1: 25 000 or 2½ INCHES to 1 MILE

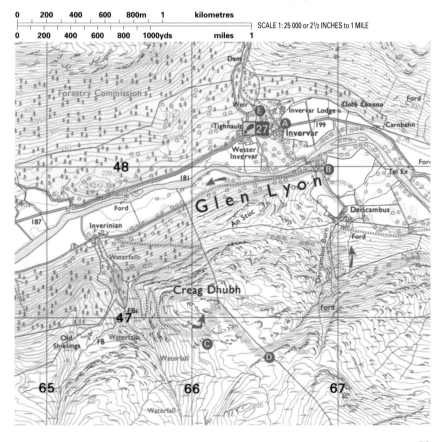

73

The way down from the summit of the rarely visited Creag Dhubh overlooking Glen Lyon

stone wall and onto a grass road running through a leafy glade of birches, oaks and rowans and on into a mixed forestry plantation. In late summer there will be mushrooms growing beside the road and also, not to be trifled with, fly agaric.

Soon Inverinian house will be seen ahead. Just before it, take the track which turns back at 45° up through the forestry. Four sharp bends and a mile (1.5 km) on, the track ends at a turning point for vehicles up on the moorland a little below the 1,818-foot (554 m) summit of Creag Dhubh. A bit of a path continues round the back of the peak for a while to an amazingly large isolated outcrop of pure white translucent quartz **(C)** lying in a bed of purple heather. It marks an area of soft ground ahead and is a good point from which to tack up the final ascent to the summit. There are actually two peaks side by side, the lesser one 14 feet (4.3 m) lower. There are also tiny peat-bogs, so care needs to be taken. To the south, three great ridges rise up to the Ben Lawers range, and east and west are possibly the best views you could find, looking obliquely down into the glen with its twisting and turning river walled in by high hills.

Return down the east side of Creag Dhubh to Invervar. Coming off the top, move south-east down beside a fence which has come up from the bottom of the glen. Before it reaches some low cliffs and starts to climb higher, leave it at right angles **(D)** to head downhill to meet a path which begins where the marshy ground drains and becomes the Dericambus Burn. The fence is best crossed by a straining-post about the diameter of a telegraph pole. Be sure to keep to the right of the burn to get onto the path, which shears away to the right before the burn drops into a ravine. The path arrives at Dericambus, goes through a gate, round the right of the farmhouse and to the aluminium gate **(B)**, passed on the ascent, which opens onto the lane to the bridge where the walk started.

Back in Invervar it is a five-minute walk up a lane on the other side of the road to the restored lint mill **(E)**. The way is well signposted, but it is not always possible to visit the mill as this is deer-stalking country. The gate to the path carries a warning of danger from bullets. ☐

28 The Cairnwell

Start:	Cairnwell Ski School
Distance:	9 miles (14.5 km)
Approximate time:	6½ hours
Parking:	Cairnwell Ski School
Refreshments:	Cairnwell Ski School (closes 5 pm)
Ordnance Survey maps:	Landranger 43 (Braemar), Pathfinder 282 NO 07/17 (Devil's Elbow)

General description *This is a walk in the sky at 3,000 feet (915 m) to climb five Munros without all the trouble of getting up there. The Old Military Road north from Spittal of Glenshee takes you up round the once notorious precipitous bends known as the Devil's Elbow to the Cairnwell Ski School at 2,296 feet (700 m). From there a chairlift, even in summer, from May to September, carries you gently up to the 2,952-foot (900 m) ridge just below The Cairnwell, a Munro of 3,060 feet (933 m). From that exhilarating height, reached by walking up only 108 feet (33 m), a vast panorama of Perthshire's highest mountains fills the western horizon, extending to the Cairngorms in the north. In summer this summit is the starting point for serious hillwalking; in winter it is the centre of Scotland's most popular skiing area. Although not closed to walkers during the winter, they must keep off the ski-slopes. Once above the chairlifts one is on high and exposed ground, so only experienced and properly equipped walkers should attempt this walk during the winter months.*

Refer to map overleaf.

Take the A93 north from Blairgowrie to the Cairnwell Ski School car park. To the west there is a deep corrie with a peak at either end, on the left The Cairnwell rising to 3,059 feet (933 m) and on the right Càrn Aosda reaching 3,007 feet (917 m). The Cairnwell Burn pours down the middle of the corrie, and there is an extremely steep path up beside it to the ridge between the two summits. But for £2 – at the time of writing – you can go up in comfort on the chairlift, or £2.50 if you want a return.

A short stroll from the top of the chairlift **(A)** to the left brings you to the top of The Cairnwell with its indicator pointing to all the major peaks that are visible, with a particularly good view down the length of Gleann Beag coming up from Spittal of Glenshee. The Cairnwell is also the starting point for a high-in-the-sky ridge walk, extending in a great curve round to the west and south.

Come off the summit by returning to the chairlift hut and head towards Càrn Aosda along the right-hand side of a fence; there are signs telling you which way to go. In the dip in the saddle, go through a gap in the fence and continue on the other side of it. The path is gravelly with large stones but makes easy walking, while the surrounding terrain is a mix of heather and grass. Near the top of the old ski-lift there is a sign stating 'Loch Vrotachan 1.1 km Cairn Aosda 1.9 km', and close by it a cairn at 2,863 feet (873 m). From there, bear left and drop down to the cairn at 2,650 feet (808 m) **(B)** above Creag a' Choire Dhirich. Then take the left hand of two paths away from Càrn Aosda to head along the top of the cliffs. It can be extremely windy along that edge, and with gusts of up to 60 mph (97 kph) it would be unwise to go too near the top of the cliff-face, which is virtually vertical.

Carn Aosda – a warning that walking Munros should be attempted only in good, settled weather

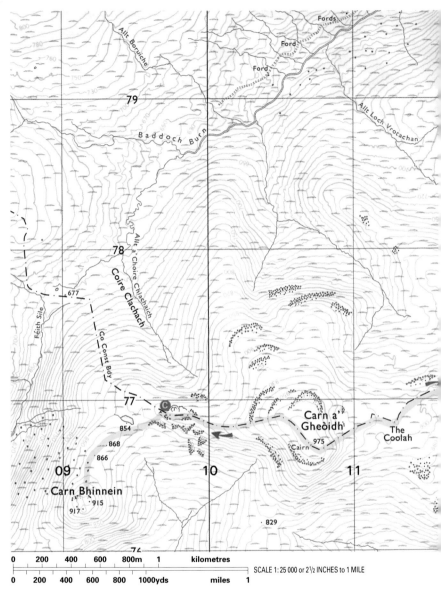

SCALE 1: 25 000 or 2½ INCHES to 1 MILE

After passing two small lochans, make for the boulder-strewn 3,017-foot (920 m) summit of Càrn nan Sac. From there the path runs west down to The Coolah, a desolate piece of ground, covered with stones and boulders and lying between two Munros, where someone has built a small cave-like shelter with room for one person.

The climb up to the 3,198-foot (975 m) Càrn a' Gheòidh starts off somewhat boggy, and in wet weather one has to pick the way carefully. At the top a small circular stone wall provides shelter from the wind. There is no longer any path to follow, and it is a question of taking a line of sight from one summit to the next over moss-covered hillsides, but sheep-paths are of some help. Climb up through rocks and boulders to a cairn (C) – not shown on the map – then make a southward curve towards the summit of Càrn Bhinnein at 3,007 feet (917 m). After long, dry spells the lochan just beyond the cairn may be no more than a dried up peat-bog. Arriving at the top of Càrn Bhinnein makes the trek well worth while. You get a view down Glen Shee with Spittal of Glenshee opening up, and all around the mountain scenery is truly magnificent.

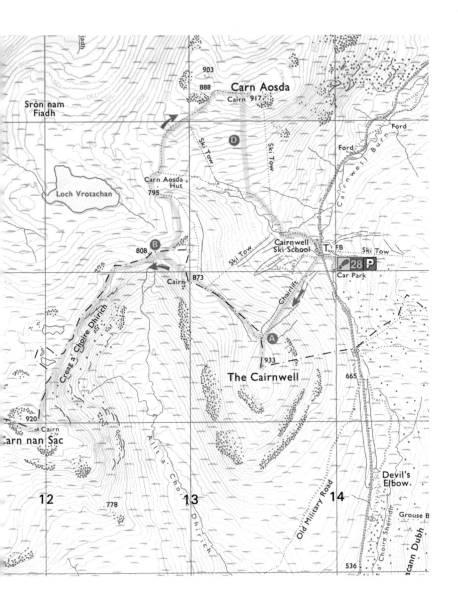

The walk now goes all the way back by the same route, but on reaching the 2,650-foot (808 m) spot height **(B)** keep on the path going north instead of returning to The Cairnwell. This climbs up past a hut to the cairned summit of Càrn Aosda. One is walking alongside the fences which mark out the *pistes* for skiers in winter; the whole face of the mountain is covered with tracks, fences and pylons for chairlifts and ski-tows. In summer they look out of place, but in winter, with the mountain cloaked in snow and the colourful figures of skiers making patterns in the snow, it is a different picture.

Up around Càrn Aosda the terrain is totally boulder- and stone-strewn, as if truckloads of ballast had been tipped there. Retreat back from the summit for about 100 yards (91 m) from where there is a path **(D)** down between the two end ski-tows. This is a quick and good way of returning to the ski school, especially if time is pressing. In summer the school complex can be a rather bleak and deserted place, its car park for 2,000 cars empty but for a handful of vehicles. It has a shop which sells souvenirs and ski gear, also a restaurant and bar, but these facilities close at 5 pm. □

Useful addresses

Forestry Commission,
231 Corstorphine Road, Edinburgh EH12 7AT.
Tel: 031 334 0303
Tay Forest District (Perthshire and Angus),
Inver Park, Dunkeld.Tel: 0350 727284

Mountaineering Council of Scotland,
16 Grosvenor Crescent Lane,
Glasgow G12 9AB.Tel: 041 334 8336
Kevin Howett, National Officer, Flat 1R,
71 King Street, Crieff. Tel: 0764 4962

Mountain rescue posts in this area:
Dounans Camp School, Aberfoyle.
Tel: 08772 291
Succoth, Arrochar. Tel: 0436 810507
Police Station, Crianlarich. Tel: 08383 222

National Trust for Scotland,
5 Charlotte Square, Edinburgh EH2 4DU.
Tel: 031 226 5922

Ordnance Survey,
Romsey Road, Maybush, Southampton SO9 4DH.
Tel: 0703 792763/4/5 or 792792

Perth and Kinross District Council,
Countryside Ranger Service,
2 High Street, Perth PH1 5PH. Tel: 0738 39911

Ramblers' Association (Scotland),
23 Crusader House, Haig Business Park,
Markinch, Fife KY7 6AQ. Tel: 0592 611177

Scottish Landowners' Federation,
25 Maritime Street, Edinburgh EH6 5PW.
Tel: 031 555 1031

Scottish Natural Heritage,
12 Hope Terrace, Edinburgh EH9 2AS.
Tel: 031 447 4784
55 York Place, Perth PH2 8EH. Tel: 0738 39746

Scottish Rights of Way Society Ltd,
Unit 2, John Cotton Business Centre,
10/2 Sunnyside, Edinburgh EH7 5RA.
Tel: 031 652 2937

Scottish Tourist Board,
23 Ravelston Terrace, Edinburgh EH4 3EU.
Tel: 031 332 2433

Scottish Wildlife Trust,
25 Johnston Terrace, Edinburgh EH1 2NH.
Tel: 031 226 4602
Visitors' Centre, Loch of Lowes, Dunkeld.
Tel: 0350 727337

Scottish Youth Hostels Association,
7 Glebe Terrace, Stirling FK8 2JA.
Tel: 0786 51181 (Hostels in this area: Perth.
Tel: 0738 23658. Pitlochry. Tel: 0796 472308)

Tourist information centres in this area (*not
open all year):
Aberfeldy, The Square. Tel: 0887 820276
*Aberfoyle, Main St. Tel: 087 72 352
Auchterarder, 90 High St. Tel: 0764 663450
Blairgowrie, 26 Wellmeadow. Tel: 0250
   872960/873701
*Callander, Rob Roy and Trossachs Visitor
   Centre, Ancaster Sq. Tel: 0877 30342
Crieff, Town Hall, High St. Tel: 0764 652578
*Dunblane, Stirling Road. Tel: 0786 824428
*Dunkeld, The Cross. Tel: 0350 727688
*Killin, Main St. Tel: 0567 8202
Perth, 45 High St. Tel: 0738 38353
Perth (Inveralmond), Caithness Glass Car
   Park, A9 West City Bypass. Tel: 0738 38481
Pitlochry, 22 Atholl Road. Tel: 0796 472215/
   472751
*Tyndrum, Main St. Tel: 083 84 246

Weather forecasts:
BBC Newsline. Tel: 0891 900 074
E. Central Scotland. Tel: 0891 500 423
E. Highlands Mountain Call. Tel: 0891 500 442
Grampians & East Highlands. Tel: 0891 500 424
National five-day forecast. Tel: 0898 500 400

Ordnance Survey maps of Perthshire

Perthshire is covered by Ordnance Survey
1:50 000 scale (2 cm to 1 km or 1¼ inches to
1 mile) Landranger sheets 42, 44, 50, 51, 54, 57,
58, 59, 65 and 66. These all-purpose maps are
packed with information to help you explore
the area. Viewpoints, picnic sites, places of
interest, caravan and campsites are shown, as
well as public rights-of-way information such
as footpaths and bridleways.
   To examine Perthshire in more detail, and
especially if you are planning walks, Ordnance
Survey Pathfinder maps at 1:25 000 scale (4 cm
to 1 km or 2½ inches to 1 mile) are ideal. Maps
covering this area are:

266 (NN 48/58) 307 (NN 45/55) 338 (NO 23/33)
267 (NN 68/78) 308 (NN 65/75) 348 (NN 62/72)
268 (NN 88/98) 309 (NN 85/95) 349 (NN 82/92)
269 (NO 08/18) 310 (NO 05/15) 350 (NO 02/12)
270 (NO 28/38) 311 (NO 25/35) 351 (NO 22/32)
279 (NN 47/57) 320 (NN 24/34) 359 (NN 61/71)

280 (NN 67/77) 321 (NN 44/54) 360 (NN 81/91)
281 (NN 87/97) 322 (NN 64/74) 361 (NO 01/11)
282 (NO 07/17) 323 (NN 84/94) 362 (NO 21/31)
283 (NO 27/37) 324 (NO 04/14) 370 (NN 60/70)
292 (NN 46/56) 325 (NO 24/34) 371 (NN 80/90)
293 (NN 66/76) 333 (NN 23/33) 372 (NO 00/10)
294 (NN 86/96) 334 (NN 43/53) 373 (NO 20/30)
295 (NO 06/16) 335 (NN 63/73) 384 (NT 09/19)
296 (NN 26/36) 336 (NN 83/93) 385 (NT 29/39)
306 (NN 25/35) 337 (NO 03/13)

   Outdoor Leisure map 3 Aviemore and the
Cairngorms covers part of Perthshire and is
also at 1:25 000 (2½ inches to 1 mile) scale.
   To get to Perthshire, use the Ordnance
Survey Travelmaster No. 1 Great Britain at
1:625 000 (1 inch to 10 miles or 1 cm to 6.25 km)
scale or Travelmaster map No. 2 Northern
Scotland, Orkney and Shetland, No. 3 Western
Scotland and the Western Isles or No. 4 Central
Scotland and Northumberland at 1:250 000
(1 inch to 4 miles or 1 cm to 2.5 km) scale.
   Perthshire is also covered on Touring Map
and Guide No.12 Scotland at 1:500 000 (1 inch
to 8 miles or 1 cm to 5 km) scale.
   Ordnance Survey maps and guides are
available from most booksellers, stationers and
newsagents.

Index